DEEP WALKING

DEEP WALKING

FOR
Body, Mind
AND
Soul

REINO GEVERS

NEW YORK

LONDON • NASHVILLE • MELBOURNE • VANCOUVER

Deep Walking
For Body Mind and Soul

Published in New York, New York, by Morgan James Publishing. Morgan James is a trademark of Morgan James, LLC. www.MorganJamesPublishing.com

ISBN 9781642798296 paperback
ISBN 9781642798302 eBook
Library of Congress Control Number: 2019914371

Cover Design by:
Rachel Lopez
www.r2cdesign.com

Morgan James is a proud partner of Habitat for Humanity Peninsula and Greater Williamsburg. Partners in building since 2006.

Get involved today! Visit
MorganJamesPublishing.com/giving-back

Dedication

To those who dare

A journey of a thousand miles begins with a single step.
– Lao Tzu

Contents

Acknowledgements

So much of the Camino experience is in the meeting of souls. This book would not have been possible without the many wonderful people I bonded with on the Camino Aragonese, the Camino del Norte, the Camino Primitivo and the Camino Frances.

The author advises readers to take full responsibility for their own safety and know their limits, before going for a walk on the Camino. Be sure that you have the right equipment and do not take risks beyond your level of experience, aptitude, training and comfort. This book is not intended as a substitute for medical advice of physicians in matters relating to health and in particular to symptoms that may require diagnosis or medical attention.

Introduction

An inner yearning harkens back to the dawn of mankind, when a species left the safety of the trees in an east African valley to start a journey on foot.

Man was in tune with the universe when feet connected with the earth and the crown of the head was aligned with the stars.

Walking upright, our ancestors followed the stars across the African continent. They crossed what is today the Strait of Gibraltar and eventually populated the globe.

The global myths and legends have a common thread in journeys of inner discovery. The story begins with an enforced exile, the undergoing of trials and tribulations on the journey itself, and finally the celebration of a victorious homecoming.

The history of mankind is woven in a matrix of countless journeys of discovery, starting with the exile of Adam and Eve from paradise.

There is a deep yearning to discover a new world within. This is one reason a growing number of spiritual seekers are rediscovering the ancient pilgrimage route in Spain—the Camino de Santiago.

A pilgrimage is much more than a hike. It can also be described as a walk to the spiritual self or God.

With the phenomenal technical progress on the exterior has come alienation within and a disconnect from nature.

Most people today live in an urban environment and in much of the Western world physical activity is limited to punching a keyboard in front of a computer screen.

Technology has made it possible for us to live longer and combat most of the diseases that wiped out much of humanity in previous generations.

Lifestyle changes in the modern world pose a different challenge. The scourges of today such as cancer, heart disease, obesity, diabetes and mental illness can be directly linked to an imbalance of the metabolism, triggered by a lack of basic exercise.

Every generation faces a different challenge. A person is destined to be in a certain place at a particular time.

The sages of old therefore encouraged their students to travel so that they would discover themselves in a foreign and sometimes alien environment.

Mastering the daily challenges faced in a different world than the everyday routine was seen as an important character-building element.

It was one of the many reasons why a pilgrimage was seen as so vital for soul-cleansing and redemption in the Middle Ages.

As one of the world's most famous pilgrimage routes, the Camino de Santiago has a long history, dating back to Celtic times, probably to the first Homo sapiens crossing to Europe from Africa.

It was so important for Christian pilgrims because the bones of St. James, one of the Apostles of Jesus, lie interred in a silver casket that can today be seen in the Cathedral of Santiago.

In recent years up to 300,000 people have walked the path annually, many of them walking the full 800 kilometers (500 miles) from St. Jean-Pied-de-Port in France to Santiago.

For every individual the motivation is different. Some are spiritual seekers; others see it as a sporting adventure. For most the decision to walk the Camino comes at a turning point in life. It may be grieving over the loss of a loved one, battling a life-threatening disease or having lost a sense of meaning or purpose.

I first walked a small section of the Camino in 2007—at the point of total physical and emotional exhaustion, with a very demanding job and dysfunctional marriage. I walked again the next year, this time a much longer section, lasting several weeks.

I only then began to understand why the Camino has become for many a modern-day route of self-discovery that can be life-transforming.

It turned out that I made some life-changing decisions after walking the Camino, like leaving a stable but unfulfilling job, severing toxic relationships and practically re-inventing my life.

After having walked thousands of kilometers on different routes of the Camino during the past decade, my conclusion is that experience—whether good or bad—will be very much a reflection of your current state of mind.

It is both a physical and a spiritual journey. Walking is one of the best and most underrated forms of exercise. It is a lower impact sport than running or going to the gym and is especially healthy for your heart, lung and body metabolism. It will at the same time improve your mood, memory and posture. More importantly you can do it anywhere and it won't cost you a thing.

A study published in the British Journal of Sports Medicine (Jan 19, 2015) found that those who adhered to a regular walking program showed significant improvements in blood pressure, slowing of resting heart rate, reduction of body fat and body weight, reduced cholesterol, improved depression scores with better quality of life and increased measures of endurance.

So why go for a walk on the Camino in Spain, and what makes it so special that hundreds of thousands of people choose to walk the path?

The Camino has a tradition going back many hundreds of years. It is a spiritual path so different from a normal hike that its uniqueness can only be perceived when you actually walk it.

After trudging for weeks through dust and rain with only a backpack, along a path walked by pilgrims, traders, soldiers and adventurers for centuries, the Camino does its own work on body and mind on a very subtle level.

If you open yourself to the magic of the Camino and walk mindfully, it will change your life.

You need not be religious or walk the entire 800 kilometers (500 miles). You can walk sections of it, but I do recommend you walk alone and on foot. Racing the path on a bicycle won't give you the same experience as taking time to see, hear and smell the magic of the moment as you walk step by step, imbibing the magic of the path.

Part of the Camino magic is the meeting of minds and the bonding experience with other pilgrims. Some of the people on the path will share intimate life stories with you. This in itself is a blessing.

Insights gathered for this book were inspired by many a long conversation with a fellow pilgrim over a glass of wine after a hard day's hike or while walking "things off."

If you are seeking an answer to some of life's greatest questions on the Camino, you might be disappointed. But the answer may also come in a very different form than you expected and some weeks after ending your walk. Few people who have walked the Camino for a lengthy period remain immune to its mystery.

God or the Universe speaks to us in many ways but we fail to listen because our awareness is clouded by the noisy chatter in a world of distraction.

When we take time for solitude, and practice alignment of the moment with the outer world and the inner self, the cracks to the soul begin to open.

For me walking is only one form of meditation.

Taking time to listen to the needs of the soul, and reawakening the senses of touch, sight and smell, widens the gaze to deeper meaning and the age-old question:

Where do I come from and where am I going?

Chapter 1

Go Lean, Go Far

O ne of the most beautiful towns on the Camino in Spain is Puenta la Reina, which translates as "Bridge of the Queen." The landscape speaks of the Roman and Arab occupations centuries ago.

Walking into the town from the Aragonese route, the pilgrim passes a mysterious building in the open countryside - the church of Santa Maria de Eunate.

Some writers date it back to the Knights Templar of the 12th century because of its similarities to the Church of the Holy Sepulchre in Jerusalem.

The octagonal shape of the inner complex, with a five-cornered exterior and a circular apse, give the place a mystical appeal.

It is surrounded by an artistic corral of stone with 33 archways decorated with figures having animal and human features. The origins of the building remain a mystery.

Exiting the town, the pilgrim walks over a beautiful old Romanesque bridge spanning the Arga river.

It also marks the convergence of the main Camino Francs route from Jean Pied le Port in France with the alternative Aragon route from Somport.

After leaving the bridge the path meanders up a steep hill where I notice a middle-aged woman with an oversized backpack. She is not doing well, perspiring and making a great effort to pull her swollen legs up the mountain. Her spectacles are dirty and fogged.

Again, I am reminded of my first walk, taking too many things I didn't need. We talk at the next bar over a café con leche (coffee with milk).

She is a high school teacher and tells me how much she had been looking forward to walking the Camino as an opportunity to destress and revitalize her life.

"I thought it would be easier. But so far, it's just been torture. I am close to giving up," she gasped, cleaning her spectacles with a dusty handkerchief

I am surprised she has made it this far. The first week of walking from St Jean-Pied-de-Port, straddling the French and Spanish border, across the rugged Pyrenees Mountains to Roncesvalles is a challenge, even for well-trained hikers.

"Your walk will be so much easier if you get yourself a smaller backpack and take a day's rest," I said, trying to be helpful.

"But I need these things," she said with gritty determination, clasping the strap of her backpack as if someone was going to take it from her.

I did not see her again. At this point you either surrender yourself to the hard realization that your feet are so blistered that it makes further walking too painful, or you take a time out to rest, dump most of the unnecessary stuff and head for the next trekking store to get a smaller backpack.

There is a saying among pilgrims of the Camino: "Be humble or the path will humble you."

On my first walk of the Camino, I had to humbly accept my first big lesson: If you carry too much unnecessary clutter, you won't get far.

The Camino is an analogy of life. You enter this world with an inhale at birth and you leave this world with an exhale. With death there is nothing you take with you but your etheric energy.

That which holds you in bondage prevents you from rising to a higher frequency of a raised consciousness and fulfilling your soul purpose.

Sometimes you just need to let go of the house you lived in for many years, the job that has become too stressful for your health and the toxic associations that keep you in an uncomfortable "comfort zone," preventing you from living out your dream.

Attachment to clutter can turn life into an unhappy state of silent misery. You fall into debt buying things that soon lose their attraction.

You wear a new set of clothing a short time before it is then forgotten in the closet. You pack a backpack for a five-week walk with stuff you don't need.

You hold onto relationships and material things that have long outlived their purpose. The two primary emotions that block you from moving forward are ANGER and FEAR!

Fear of rejection is the emotion that makes you want to compete with the Joneses, trying to impress the people you least like. It is the innate fear of dying of hunger, thirst and cold, that makes you fill your back pack with rubbish you don't need.

The difficulty in letting things go is that whispering fear in the subconscious mind:

"I might still need it one day!"

Yet, the modern-day Camino is a walk in the park in comparison to what the pilgrims in the Middle Ages had to endure.

Many of them did not survive the walk that took them from their doorstep in Holland, Poland, Germany or England, lasting many months, even years. They were confronted by innumerable obstacles including disease, injury from wild animals and robbers.

The Camino is dotted with stone crosses marking the sites where the pilgrims of old died along the way. Some are several hundred years old; others are fairly recent.

Coming into Spain on the Aragonese route to the town of Jaca, the hiker passes excavations of a massive medieval hospital where nuns took care of pilgrims who had just crossed from the Pyrenees mountains.

In modern-day Spain there is a bar or café that awaits the pilgrim with refreshments in every town and village at about 10-kilometer (6.2 miles), sometimes 5- kilometer (3.1 mile), intervals. A taxi can be ordered from anywhere to take you to the next town if you find that you are reaching your physical limit. Taxis will even transport your backpack to the next town.

Pilgrims rush to rise from their bunk beds in the early hours of the morning, afraid they might not get a bed in the next town—still stuck in the fear of stressed-out and anxious lives.

Most fears are mental illusions that hardly ever materialize into reality.

Thoughts come to mind as I recollect that pain of each blister with every step and the weight of my backpack rubbing against my back and shoulders on my first walk.

My low-priced backpack is coming loose at the straps and my boots are sub-standard.

Lesson number one:

"Don't scrimp on the essentials."

The slow realization dawns. You are never going to make it to Santiago like this.

Fast-track back to the days just before the journey began.

Several people I knew at the time had walked the entire Camino from St. Jean-Pied-de Port, traversing the steep Pyrenees mountains, the plains of the Meseta, the vineyards of the Rioja valley and the green hills of Galicia.

"If they can do it, I can do it too," I said to myself.

The first mistake. Every individual is different. Preparation for any journey, project or objective is key. I was handicapped by a foot that was shattered from a fall of several meters from a tree at the age of fourteen with a bone missing in the second toe. A longer walk forced me to slow my pace to a painful limp.

A young Australian woman urged me on: "Just keep on walking the things off," she said. The big surprise came some days later when the pain I had been dealing with for years simply disappeared. My walk became so much easier and I had hardly finished my first short Camino when I was already making plans to do a longer walk the next year, this time more prepared.

If you don't know how far you are going or where you are going, you will be confronted by many obstacles and eventually give up in frustration.

The bottom line: Make a checklist of the essentials and ask yourself these questions:

Do I really, really need this?

Have I used or worn this during the past six months? If not, there is a high probability that you don't really need it.

On the Camino the essentials are a good backpack, high-quality worn-in boots, two pairs of hiking socks, a warm rain jacket, T-shirt, a second pair of underwear, lightweight sleeping bag and the basic toiletry items.

Our consumer-oriented society brainwashes us round the clock with the message that we need this or that thing to be happy.

Take a "happy pill" to get rid of that feeling of despondency. There is a pill for everything. Society indoctrinates us that we always need to be happy and healthy.

But sometimes we just need to live through that sadness or that pain to move to the next level of consciousness.

The rude awakening comes when the drug wears off and we find we can't live without it.

We get that new dress or that new car and are disappointed. Then we get the next thing, and fall into an endless pit of debt.

Letting go of the things down to the bare essentials sharpens the realization that happiness is not dependent on what you own.

An internal emptiness can never be compensated by external means.

Happiness is a state of mind, a thought process and a state of BEING. Part of the happiness of BEING is simply to be grateful for what we already have.

Thoughts of the past and the future are just thoughts. Walking in the moment and practicing being completely in the moment opens the senses to who we are, to God, the universal intelligence or the higher BEING.

A pilgrimage on the Camino is walking off that which is weighing you down and finding soul purpose. With every step you are walking into and onto the path of becoming who you really are.

But it need not be only the Camino in Spain. The Camino might be on your bucket list of once-in-a-lifetime experiences if you live far outside of Europe.

If you train yourself to be conscious and aware, however, any walk in nature, anywhere on our beautiful planet, can become your inner Camino of self-discovery.

The Essentials

- What stuff haven't you worn or used during the past six months?
- What attachments do you have to the stuff that no longer serves your higher purpose?
- Keep the memories. You don't need to keep the item.
- What relationship, activity or mindset has outlived itself?
- Happiness is a state of BEING rather than a state of HAVING.
- You go farther by making yourself lean and reducing what you need to the ESSENTIALS.

Chapter 2

Walking the Rollercoaster

Will the day control your agenda or will you be in control of your day? Are you in control of your thoughts and emotions or do your feelings and emotions control you?

The first thought of the day when getting up in the morning determines your day. Have a bad dream and a bad thought and you will most likely be grumpy all day.

Transmute a bad thought or feeling with a good thought or say a good prayer and you most likely will have a good day.

You will instantly know your thoughts when you close your eyes and examine how you are feeling now.

Are you feeling happy, sad or angry? External circumstances are not under your control but you can control your thoughts and reactions to them and transmute negative thoughts into positive flow.

The perfect antidote to a bad start in your day is to implement a daily gratitude ritual. What are the three things in your life that you are truly grateful for? What did I experience the day before that made me truly happy and grateful that I am alive and well?

The wheel of life goes through cycles of ups and downs. The first section of the walk on the Camino is a steep climb in the Pyrenees Mountains. It is described as the Path of Crucifixion.

Questions and doubts may arise as the first blisters start hurting your feet and your body starts its rebellion against an unfamiliarly hard challenge: Why am I doing this? Weather in this part of northwestern Spain can be unpredictable, with cold winds and rain lashing your body.

The Meseta, an endless flatland between Burgos and Astorga, is seen as the valley of death, especially in the summer months when the heat, the dust, the thirst and the boring flat countryside can be too much. Many pilgrims therefore choose to avoid this stretch, instead taking a bus or a different route.

Other pilgrims who persisted through the valley of death describe it as an essential part of the Camino experience.

After this stretch the walk gets much easier. The pilgrim has been on the road for several weeks and has walked through the most difficult stretches and blisters. Walking gets easier and he or she might find that walking for 25 or 30 kilometers a day is not really a big deal. The path of resurrection or rebirth is felt all the way to the final destination in Santiago.

Despite the many glossy travel reports and guide books, the Camino has its shadow sides. Some sections of the Path are crowded with day tourists. Groups of cyclists show little regard for a slow-walking pilgrim with a backpack as they come up fast behind you and expect you to give way, persistently ringing their bicycle bell.

Sleeping in a bunk bed in an albergue, or hostel, with at least a dozen other pilgrims, half of them keeping you awake with loud snoring, will not particularly improve your mood.

One of my worst nights on the Camino was spending a night in a bunk bed of an overcrowded room with the air thick from the smell of sweat and dust. Most of us had slept badly, with several snoring pilgrims keeping us awake.

"I will report this albergue to the authorities. These conditions are simply unacceptable," a middle-aged and bleary-eyed German woman snapped while packing her backpack the next morning.

I noticed that several other pilgrims moved away from her. The others were simply trying to make the best of the situation. As we moved out into the garden, we were greeted by a spectacular sunrise, with the light glittering over the river in front of us.

For most of us the bad night was instantly forgotten, while the woman was still whining and complaining.

Staying in a dark mood will sometimes make you miss one of the yellow way markers as you start your walk in an unfamiliar environment, losing your way, forcing you to make a U-turn and walking much longer than you had planned.

Walking alone for many hours can reawaken old emotional demons, that unfinished business going back many years that you had thought you had dealt with a long time ago.

Do you let a toxic emotion like anger, hatred or envy pass? Or do you cling to it and let it spoil your day?

Do you let the sadness over the "good old days," over those things that are no more, overshadow your ability to experience the moment?

I have always experienced my first few days on the Camino as a challenge, as if the universe itself was testing my determination to actually walk those many kilometers still lying ahead.

You will have the cycles of ups and downs every day as you walk. The "positive-thinking-stay-happy culture" with which we are bombarded daily by the glossy lifestyle magazines does not reflect life's reality.

Trying to switch to "happy" when we are sad doesn't work and is not authentic. The first step is in honestly accepting how you feel. The challenge is then to not stay in that negative mode and to find a way to the reset button.

I am convinced that those people who are happiest and most content with their lives are those people who have found a coping strategy of dealing with the ever-changing fortunes of the wheel of life.

Some of the world's most successful people have had terrible down cycles and tragedies to deal with in their lives. Nelson Mandela, who spent many years of a life sentence in solitary confinement and hard labor on Robben Island, sustained himself with the dream that he would one day be president of a democratic South Africa.

Billionaire Richard Branson admitted in his autobiography that the first 15 years of his airline were "a topsy-turvy tale of excitement, innovation and survival."

From the outside we often tend to look only at the fruits of the highly successful, not seeing the numerous failures, disappointments and huge efforts that formed the building blocks of their fortune and fame.

Winston Churchill, who sustained the British people during World War II, when everything seemed lost, wrote:

"Success is stumbling from failure to failure with no loss of enthusiasm."

When starting your walk on the Camino, it can seem a daunting task to walk more than 800 kilometers (500 miles) through Spain with a nothing more than a backpack, carrying the essentials.

When hitting a down cycle you appreciate all the more the joy and gratitude of the up cycle. It is within this law of opposites that insight and wisdom grow that we can accept with humility those things we cannot change. All that we can change is our attitude and mindset toward them.

Companionship with other pilgrims is extremely helpful in facing the emotional and physical challenges on the Camino. A conversation with a fellow pilgrim can be a helpful distraction in the early part of the walk as you battle the challenge of dealing with your body adapting to a walk of several hours each day.

I've found that these conversations have seldom been mundane, with pilgrims soon revealing their inner feelings and reasons for being on the Camino.

There is soon a heart-to-heart connection and trusting relationship that one only has with friends or family members one has known for many years in the real world.

I've found the penniless Spanish student, retired Dutch school teacher, successful French entrepreneur, American university professor, Italian clergyman, and world traveler from South Korea conversing around a dinner table as if they have known each other for years.

It is one of the deeper mysteries of the Camino that has drawn me back to this journey on foot more than a dozen times.

The Essentials

- Are you in control of your thoughts and emotions?
- Do you start your day with a positive anchor?
- The antidote to a negative mindset is gratitude.
- If you have the feeling that life has dealt you a bad set of cards, keep in mind: The wheel of life keeps turning. "This too shall pass."
- Failure and hardship are preconditions to success!
- Appreciate the moment. It will make you feel alive.

Chapter 3

Deep Walking

You stand on a cliff overlooking the ocean. Wind moves dark clouds, opening to sunlight, illuminating the ocean with its gentle waves glittering as if decorated by innumerable gemstones. That is when you feel that incredible feeling of solitude and peace, and the gratitude of the moment. A change of perspective and the world appears in radiant colors.

You are at one and feel integrated with that invisible matrix. Within is as Without. It is discovering the inner Christ or the inner Buddha. The Creator, the Universe, God is not a separate entity but that which is Being.

The first days of walking are a push against mental and physical obstacles. After going through this tunnel of resistance, you feel that inner peace that comes with deep walking.

Deep walking on a pilgrimage is a journey toward the heart of inner consciousness step by step, day by day and week by week.

You feel that revitalizing energy flow in your body as you release the heavy treadmill of past and future thoughts in your head.

When you are no longer at war with yourself, body, mind and soul fall into alignment. You appreciate the beauty of a sunset, the beaming farmer greeting you with a friendly "Hola," the chimes of the sheep bells ringing in your ears, and the rushing waters of a crystal-clear stream of mountain water.

The Camino del Norte, the northern coastal route of the Camino, starts in the Basque city of Bilbao, taking the pilgrim along a coastline dotted with sleepy fishing villages and beautiful beaches.

Battling at times rough weather with cold, rainy winds from the Bay of Biscay whipping our faces, I walked this section with my good friend Tom.

The month of May in this part of Spain can bring you a beautiful warm spring day or a rough day with wind and rain.

Then you ask yourself when you will finally reach the next town, trudging through muddy paths with raindrops dripping onto your shivering body.

And yet when you stand on a cliff experiencing that magical moment, you know that it has all been worth it.

Scientists have meanwhile found that exposure to blue spaces such as lakes, rivers and the sea is particularly beneficial to mental health.

A team from the Barcelona Institute for Global Health (ISGlobal) undertook the first international review of 35 studies on "blue spaces."

Their conclusion: Outdoor blue spaces not only reduced stress levels but also improved the feeling of general well-being and physical activity.

Similar studies have also been undertaken on "green spaces." Nature and the sounds of nature have a healing effect on the human body.

When I stood on that cliff overlooking the ocean, I felt relaxed, at ease and reenergized for the first time in months.

Mindfulness of the wonders of the natural world around us seems to brings a natural order to chaotic thoughts and emotions.

"Blue and green spaces" happen when your entire being is cleansed by the soothing sounds of waves crashing to shore, the salty smell of seawater penetrating your nostrils and you hear the gentle wind blowing through the green pasture next to you.

Juergen was walking very slowly because of a knee problem. He had analyzed for himself why he had been forced by the path to slow down:

"I was trying to go too fast, seeing it all like a physical exercise routine that had to be accomplished in a certain time."

We didn't see Juergen for a couple of days, until we were having our café con leche on a balcony overlooking a beautiful beach in the city of Gijon.

"Surely that can't be Juergen," I said to Tom. "He was way behind us." It sure was Juergen, looking very downcast and limping badly on the beach below us.

Juergen's face brightened immediately upon seeing our familiar faces. It turned out that he had decided at that moment walking the beach to end his walk and to return home.

After we had a good meal together, Juergen changed his mind. His knee pain improved and he continued the walk with us all the way to Santiago.

Juergen kept a meticulous diary each day on the many lessons he had learned on the Camino, and like so many of us who have walked the path, he turned his life around after getting back home.

At the time he was walking the Camino he was still running a tough business and needed out.

At the time of our walk on the Camino del Norte in May of 2008, the number of good pilgrims' hostels was relatively sparse.

On one particular day the three of us walked some 35 kilometers (21.7 miles) in drenching rain to the next village, where we were told we could find accommodation.

We walked through several deserted villages, and then a long, winding country road. The last part of a journey is often the most difficult. At every turn we expected to reach our destination, only to find another hill to cross.

Finally, as darkness began to set in, the rain still pouring incessantly, we reached the town. The only hotel was locked with an "en venta" (for sale) signpost in the window.

A granny walking her dog pointed ahead. "El albergue esta recto." (The albergue is straight ahead.)

We had to walk another two kilometers to a place outside town, where we finally found the faded signpost: "albergue peregrine."

"This does not look promising," I said to the others.

Our hearts sank when we entered the building. The roof was leaking. Mold was all over the walls and ceiling. The previous occupants had left dirty dishes and rancid food in the kitchen. The beds were moist.

"Never will I sleep in this place," Tom said.

"Well, I guess we'll have to sleep under a bridge," I responded.

As we picked up our backpacks, I noticed a card on the door: "Albergue Privado" (private hostel), with a telephone number.

"Yes, there is still accommodation available," the person on the other end of the line said. But it was another five kilometer walk for three exhausted pilgrims.

But what we found exceeded all our expectations. We were put up in a beautiful home overlooking the ocean with a crackling fireplace, giving us that comforting home feeling that we had been missing for weeks.

Sometimes the universe rewards in unexpected ways when we are open to accept the gift. It compensated for every hardship and disappointment we had to endure that day.

We fell asleep, each in his own comfortable bedroom, with the surf of the nearby ocean guiding us into sleep.

Before reaching Santiago we had more challenges coming our way. We got hopelessly lost in a forest, the path becoming more sparsely and badly signposted as we went along.

We retraced our steps backward, then decided to go forward again. We checked our maps and were even more confused because the description in the guide book didn't match any of the landmarks we were seeing.

At the moment of despair and hopelessness we heard footsteps. A woman with a toothless grin, red cheeks and a bag of firewood on her back seemed just as surprised to find fellow humans at this remote spot.

"Estamos perdidos (We are lost)," I said.

"Don't worry," she replied. "Down the hill and follow the river. Buen Camino."

The universe "always offers a solution, when you really want it," Juergen said dryly.

"And there will always be people coming your way to point you into the right direction," I said.

In the days before we reach Santiago there is an unspoken agreement. We walk together but separately, each with his own impressions, thoughts and perspectives.

Juergen sees a lot of butterflies flying his way, which he says are teaching him to be more carefree and easygoing. Tom avoids treading on countless lizards. It is a hardy animal that can adapt to any circumstance. I see and hear blackbirds everywhere, teaching me to appreciate their beauty of song and to trust my intuition.

We sleep in dirty, crowded hostels that test every mental boundary. Our feet are hurting with blisters. We are followed by aggressively barking dogs. We walk through sleepy villages and pass through deserted farmyards.

Beyond the basic needs of eating, drinking and sleeping, the spiritual teachings from the universe pave their way through the subconscious mind, layer by layer. A bird song, a word from a passing pilgrim, the ruins of an old chapel, the stained features of the Madonna carved in stone trigger images, thoughts and feelings.

Chapter 4

Magic of the Moment

If you wait for the perfect moment when all is safe and assured,
it may never arrive. Mountains will not be climbed,
races won, or lasting happiness achieved.
– Maurice Chevalier

Happiness is a state of "Being" and not something to be achieved. Yet, we are bombarded daily with subliminal messages and images that feed the mind with negative messages.

If you are dreaming of the things you have always wanted to do in life, postponing them to some distant day when you retire, and always finding excuses like lack of money, then your dreams will most likely stay dreams forever.

19

Taking concrete action, saving just a little cash for that once-in-a-lifetime trip, informing yourself through literature about your secret destination will inevitably make your dream come true.

When taking time out for a longer walk, the "things" we were chasing in the daily rut become irrelevant. Yes, we need to be able to provide for basic needs like shelter, food and clothing. But most of the other things our mind is preoccupied with are not that important in the bigger picture when we refocus on soul purpose and meaning.

We are constantly being pulled away from the task at hand. Multi-tasking is expected and common in most workplaces. Psychologists have found that distraction is a major cause of unhappiness.

Psychologists at Harvard University conducted a study with 2,250 volunteers, monitoring their thoughts and feelings, to find out how often they were focused on what they were doing, and what made them most happy.

More than half the time people's minds were wandering to other things. The researchers concluded that reminiscing, thinking ahead or daydreaming tends to make people more miserable, even when they are thinking about something pleasant.

Matthew Killingsworth, a doctoral student in psychology and lead author of the study, wrote in the journal *Science*:

"A human mind is a wandering mind and a wandering mind is an unhappy mind. The ability to think about what is not happening is a cognitive achievement that comes at an emotional cost."

While walking the Camino, I have repeatedly found myself daydreaming about things from the past or the future. On my first Camino I was hardly on the path for the first two hours when I missed the first yellow way mark, walking right past it until an observant farmer on the field waved to me.

"Hola, hola." He gestured with a loud, "Santiago! Santiago," to retrace my steps to the last marker.

It was one of my first lessons: Stay in the moment. Getting lost in mountains at dusk when temperatures can fall rapidly has in recent years claimed the lives of several hikers in Spain.

Watch a dog chasing a ball on the beach or a bird looking for insects in the grass and you soon realize that for all other species living in the moment is a natural phenomenon. It's just that we humans seem to have enormous difficulty in staying fully present.

Humans are hard-wired to live in the past or in the future because planning and learning from the past has been crucial to the survival of our species.

Real joy comes from those magical moments of being absolutely present and experiencing spirituality, love and peace of mind.

It is an enlightening experience to "listen" to your own thoughts when walking. Becoming aware of your thoughts is the first step toward focusing on the moment.

It is an empowering thought to realize that you are in control of your thoughts and that with a little training you can regain control of the monkeys dancing in in the head.

We can be trained to anchor the mind to the present moment. The modern human brain suffers from information overload so that our mind starts sifting and dropping information it finds unnecessary. If your attention is focused on an event going back weeks or months, you will not appreciate the nature around you. You will miss way markers and get lost.

A growing body of research shows that our attention span in the digital world is rapidly declining. We appear to take our mind away from the task at hand about 50 percent of our waking hours, time travelling to the past or the future.

It becomes a problem when the mind gets distracted by fears and worries about things that seldom ever happen in reality.

Training the mind to be fully in the present takes practice, much like starting a physical exercise routine. You become better at it the more you repeat it.

Mindful walking, or treading the ground softly, is one method. Slow down your walking to your breathing rhythm, lifting a foot with an in-breath and placing in on the ground with an out-breath.

I also find the first pattern in the tai chi movement, the "awakening of the chi," very helpful.

With each exhaling breath you align the center of both feet to a point deep in the center of the earth. Then you feel that energy rise from the earth through your feet and up your spine to the top of your head. You then align the top of your head with heaven above. With each inhaling breath you lift your arms to shoulder height feeling the connection to heaven and with each exhaling breath you lower your arms down to your thighs feeling that grounding to mother earth.

Another technique is to repeat a mantra. My favorite one is OM MANI PADME HUM, repeating it 108 times and then repeating again until you feel that you are once more aligned.

Hindus believe OM is the mystic vibration of the supreme, that original first creative sound that emanated from the universe, representing the divinity in the past, present and future. It is seen as that sourcing sound, connecting and joining all things.

Proponents of the Big Bang theory believe that the universe was not really created by a "bang" but more like the humming sound of OM.

The chanting of OM or AUM, especially in a group, has an enormously calming effect and vibrational healing effect on the body. I've seen pilgrims chanting it on the Camino to great effect.

The powerful vocal intonation of A has a broader effect on the conscious state of mind, the U reaches out to the calm dreamlike state of the unconscious, and the M is the reverberating vibration felt throughout the body and deep within the brain.

Walkers or bikers on the Camino miss the point by rushing from one destination to the next, or constantly looking at their smart phone while the world passes them by.

There is yearning for solitude and peace of mind but obviously they find great difficulty switching off from the stressed-out treadmill of life and continue in the same mode on the Camino.

Take a break, savor the nature around you by opening your sense of smell to the herbs by the wayside, open your ears to the chorus of bird song and feel that cool mountain breeze caressing your face.

Nature is the best healer!

At least for some sections of your journey on the Camino, I recommend you walk alone to truly appreciate how the Camino slowly works at healing body and mind. Most pilgrims on the way respect each other's need either for company or for solitude.

Learning to appreciate solitude, enduring through those moments of accepting SELF will gradually open consciousness to the wisdom of the universe.

The Essentials

- Happiness is in appreciating the moment.
- Avoid distraction by concentrating on one thing at a time.
- Staying in the moment can be learned. You get better the more you train.
- Nature is the best healer if you open all your senses to her magic.

Chapter 5

Meditation

J ust take a walk alone and realize how much your mind starts wandering after only a few minutes.

The average person has between 50,000 and 70,000 thoughts per day, which translates to between 35 and 48 thoughts per minute.

The number obviously varies with every individual but the mind is constantly making decisions for you and seldom do you realize how much you jump from one thought to the next.

In our digital age we are bombarded with information that creates the illusion that we will be happier if we accumulate more things and that we "know it all."

Most of the news we hear and see is of a negative nature. Some people know more about the lives of the rich and famous than of the neighbor next door.

If we reflect closely on our thoughts, we will most likely agree that most of them are negative and find their root in hurts of the past or fears of the future.

There is abundant research on our stressful lives that indicates stress always starts with a thought. The mind hardware is wired to focusing on the negative. It is part of our survival instinct that has made us so addicted to negative news.

Having worked in the media industry for many years I know how difficult it is to catch a reader's attention with positive news.

The more dramatic, bloody and sensational your headline, the more readers.

It is that part of the reptilian brain that comes into play here, telling us homo sapiens to gather as much information about our surroundings to avoid possible injury or death.

But a volcano outbreak in Indonesia has little relevance to someone living in South Dakota. Mass media is driven by the vibration of catastrophe and fear—which in turn reflects a need of society.

We have been given the freedom of choice. Some researchers believe we react subconsciously to the information we digest, more or less becoming victims of mass propaganda.

But another body of research, from the school of positive psychology, argues that we can literally transform our lives with mental discipline.

We know from our own lives that a day dominated by constant whining and negativity—especially from family members and work colleagues–makes us feel drained and exhausted.

In contrast, when we give a person a compliment, and we are surrounded by loving caring people, we feel physically our energy expanding around our heart and body.

We are imperfect beings and cannot escape the human condition. All the major religions know this and have created ritual, meditation, prayer and recitation as means of mind control.

The downside is that religion has hijacked spirituality and very often replaced it with dogma, intolerance, lack of compassion, unkindness and fundamentalism.

For centuries religion has told us that if we do this and don't do that, we are on the right track. Meanwhile the veil has fallen. The church or religion is as much in crisis mode as are so many other institutions entrenched in the social fabric.

The bigotry behind so much of institutionalized religion has in recent years surfaced in the form of sexual abuse, abuse of power, financial irregularities and much more.

Religion is a necessary precondition to the elevation of spiritual consciousness. It can only be the exterior form or offer the tools toward individual spiritual experience.

More than ever before, there is a deep need for the quietness of the mind. Only in that empty space of complete presence can we perceive the voice of our innermost being.

Meditation has been an integral part of the spiritual journey for thousands of years. There are different forms in every religious practice. In essence, it is practicing discipline of thought.

The human condition is constantly pulling us into those thoughts of meanness, self-doubt, retribution and hate. These thoughts in turn trigger action and create what the Buddhists call "negative karma"—the law of cause and effect.

One of the simplest means of meditation is just focusing the mind on deep breathing, counting as we inhale and exhale. It can be done by sitting in the lotus position, on a chair or while doing a walking meditation.

Extensive research has established beyond doubt the positive effects of meditation, on both the mental and physical levels.

A Harvard study found that meditating over an eight- week period has a powerful impact on regions of the brain associated with stress, empathy and sense of self.

Magnetic resonance (MR) images were taken of the brain structure of 16 study participants two weeks before and after they took part in an eight-week Mindfulness-Based Stress Reduction (MBSR) Program at the University of Massachusetts Center for Mindfulness.

In addition to weekly meetings that included practice of mindfulness meditation—which focuses on nonjudgmental awareness of sensations, feelings, and state of mind—participants received audio recordings for guided meditation practice and were asked to keep track of how much time they practiced each day.

The participants practiced an average of 27 minutes of mindfulness training per day. An analysis of the brain scans found increased gray matter density in the hippocampus part of the brain, known to be important for structures associated with self-awareness, compassion and introspection.

The art of tai chi—often described as meditation in motion—was found to have similar positive health effects.

"A growing body of carefully conducted research is building a compelling case for tai chi as an adjunct to standard medical treatment for the prevention and rehabilitation of many conditions commonly associated with age," says Peter M. Wayne, assistant professor of medicine at Harvard Medical School.

Researchers from the Institute of Integral Qigong and Tai Chi in Santa Barbara, California, Arizona State University, and the University of North Carolina analyzed 77 articles reporting the results of 66 randomized controlled trials of tai chi and qi gong. The studies involved a total of 6,410 participants.

Of the many outcomes identified by the researchers, the strongest evidence of health benefits for tai chi or qi gong relates to bone health, cardiopulmonary fitness, balance and factors associated with preventing falls, quality of life, and self-efficacy.

Other body arts such as yoga were also found to significantly reduce stress hormones in the body such as cortisol.

Yoga is a form of mind-body fitness that involves a combination of muscular activity and an internally directed mindful focus on awareness of the self, the breath, and energy.

Consistent practice of yoga was found to improve depression and can lead to significant increases in serotonin levels, coupled with decreases in the levels of monamine oxidase, an enzyme that breaks down neurotransmitters and the stress hormone cortisol (McCall, T. New York: Bantam Dell, a division of Random House Inc; 2007. *Yoga as Medicine*).

We are only beginning to understand the positive effects the ancient body arts of tai chi and yoga, practiced in India and China for thousands of years, on the well-being of body mind and spirit.

The advantage of deep walking is that you can do it anywhere. You can start by re-programming your mind into the fully present deep walking mode as you walk from the car park or train station to work.

Meditative walking is possible anywhere. Only 15 minutes of deep walking every day of every week, of every month will soon have a profoundly positive effect on body, mind and soul.

The Essentials

- Discipline your thoughts: Are they predominantly happy or negative thoughts?
- Find the form of meditation best suited for your needs: It could be a prayer, a mantra, or a breathing or body exercise.
- Mind-body fitness can be trained with yoga, tai chi, qigong or deep walking exercises.
- Body and mind are one. If you control your thoughts in whatever you do, you will enhance your health and well-being.

Chapter 6

Persistence

Gerrit is gentle giant with a winning smile and natural friendliness toward everyone he meets. He walks with a steady staccato rhythm, having come a long way when I meet him some 200 kilometers (124 miles) from Santiago.

He stops at one of the crosses at the wayside that marks a spot where a pilgrim many hundreds of years ago died.

"This is the best way to die. Boom, up and straight to heaven," he chuckles with a wide grin across his sunburned face.

"You are not planning to die right now, are you?" I ask, looking him up and down to check if he is having a seizure.

"Not right now, I can assure you. I am planning to make it to Santiago," he says.

I feel a sense of relief, for Gerrit is a man well into his 80s—one of the many examples of people I met on the Camino who exemplified persistence in every sense of the word. As humans we are capable of far more than our mind leads to believe.

Gerrit had this pilgrimage on his bucket list for a long time. He was going to do the Camino like the pilgrims of old, walking from the doorstep of his apartment in Amsterdam to Santiago by foot, despite a range of health issues from heart to back problems and a bad limp from an injury many years ago.

Defying all the odds and going against the advice of friends and family, he began his 2000-kilometer (1242 mile) journey to Santiago de Compostela, taking it very slow at first, doing eight to ten kilometers a day. He meets locals and people on the way who open their home to the old man to stay the night. Sometimes he even sleeps in a barn or outdoors while walking through France, where there are far less pilgrims' hostels than in Spain. Other times he knocks on the door of the local parish, showing his pilgrim's pass, the credential, asking for a bed for the night.

After several weeks on the Camino Gerrit easily walks his 25 kilometers (15.5 miles) a day, outpacing many a hiker half his age.

"No, that can't be. You can't be that old and walked the Camino all the way from Amsterdam?" is written all over their faces.

I met Gerrit again some days later at the Cathedral in Santiago, grinning from ear to ear, holding the certificate in his hands that certified that he had walked the entire Camino on foot.

I've met numerous people like Gerrit on the Camino who have often been surprised at themselves at what the human body and mind are really capable of doing. We constantly underestimate our true capabilities. People have done the Camino walking barefoot, in a wheelchair, or pushing a baby in a pram. Highly trained athletes have been running it on an average of almost 70 kilometers (43.5 miles) a day.

Faith in the biblical sense can truly move mountains. Theresa decides to walk the Camino in an act of defiance after her doctor tells her that the cancer in her body will reduce her lifespan to six months at the most and that she should settle her affairs.

She walks the Camino with soft feet, sending her backpack ahead to the next town with a taxi. She completes her walk and returns home a different woman.

"That was five years ago," she tells me as we drink our café con leche in one of the many bars dotting the Camino. This time she is walking the Camino the second time.

Theresa and Gerrit prove that spirit is more powerful than the body—and there are countless similar stories of people overcoming almost insurmountable obstacles.

We are only at the infant stage of discovering the true connection between body and mind.

The Austrian-born Jewish psychiatrist Victor Frankl (1905-1997) is renowned for his breakthrough research on the power of meaning. In his book *Nevertheless, Say "Yes" to Life: A Psychologist Experiences the Concentration Camp,* also known under the bestselling title *Man's Search for Meaning,* he narrates several observations in the Nazi death camps.

While incarcerated in Auschwitz, Frankl counselled fellow prisoners with his philosophy that a striving for meaning, even in the most harrowing of circumstances, is what keeps us alive.

Inmates who gave themselves up became suicidal and died, while those who saw some meaning, like telling the world about the Holocaust after liberation, survived.

It was the *"will to meaning"* that looked to the future, and not to the traumatic events of the past, that sustained people.

Despite losing his wife and nearly all his family in the holocaust, Frankl refused to dwell on the past.

Even in the worst possible situation, man still has freedom of choice and the ability to seek meaning in whatever situation he finds himself in, he argued.

"Everything can be taken from a *man* but one thing: the last of the human freedoms—to choose one's attitude in any given set of circumstances, to choose one's own way," he wrote.

It's a simple but profound truth. It all begins in the mind.

It is why a cancer patient will very often give up when told of the diagnosis. The word itself is so loaded with fear and mortality that the patient sees no hope. The shocked reaction of family and friends is often not conducive to the healing process either, when the patient is asked on a daily basis how "the cancer treatment is going."

We also know from research that patients who overload their friends and family on a daily basis with all the details of their illness do much worse than those who refuse to mention by name the illness, merely telling everyone that they are in a healing process. Most fitness and weight-loss programs fail because of a negative mindset.

After an initial loss of weight or a couple of exercise sessions, most people give up and return to old habits because they haven't found the real reason in their mind why they want to reduce weight or get fit. Some people even end up being more obese because they have subconsciously tricked their mind into putting on more weight. "I don't want to be fat. I don't want to be in debt," are a double-negative with opposite the intended effect.

Reformulating that wish into a realistic feeling that is actually felt as an emotion and pictured as an ideal outcome really works. It has been tested successfully by countless people who have studied Jack Canfield's book *Chicken Soup for the Soul*, or Rhonda Byrne's bestseller, *The Secret*.

Both Gerrit and Theresa practiced this on the Camino, picturing in their mind prior to starting the walk each day how they walked effortlessly step by step to the next destination, even where they would be spending the next night.

Toxic emotions such as anger and fear will inevitably draw what you don't want into your life. If these emotions do appear, as they inevitably do all the time, practice reframing them into positive energy such as gratitude for all the good things that have come into your life.

The Essentials

- Persistence is practicing the mind.
- Spirit is much more powerful than the body.
- The little steps done repeatedly and with consistency will make you achieve your goal.
- Set a realistic target first before you move on to the next challenge.
- Negative emotions are poison to persistence and goal-setting. Reframe your mind into picturing the positive outcome you intend to achieve.

Chapter 7
The Holy Grail

In the Middle Ages Europe was a conglomeration of different kingdoms and fiefdoms.

On the Camino the pilgrim will repeatedly come across towns and villages that might instill the feeling that one has walked back in time.

Along the Aragonese route of the Camino, near Jaca, there is a remarkable ancient building built into a rocky outcrop.

The monastery of San Juan de la Pena dates to the ninth century and for a time it was the spiritual and intellectual heart of the Kingdom of Aragon.

Monasteries such as San Juan de la Pena were the Silicon Valleys of medieval times, financed generously by the kingdoms competing with each other across Europe.

They laid the foundations of modern astronomy, art, literature and science. Behind the monastery walls the intellects of the time could fully focus on their endeavors, freed from the constraints of hard labor to pro-vide for food and shelter.

It was curse and a blessing. The research was embedded in the sacred and religious structure of the day. It was prohibited by religious doctrine to dissect the human body, preventing medical advance for centuries.

The modern dilemma is that science has on the one hand brought us within one generation unimaginable advances like the smart phone and the MRT body scan. On the other hand, it has brought the world to an ecological brink and all human life could be annihilated at the touch of a nuclear button.

The monasteries of the Middle Ages were not only research centers but focal points of prayer and pilgrimage. The more pilgrims, the more income and the more precious the relic dating back to the time of Jesus and his apostles, the more pilgrims: it was a simple formula that worked for centuries in helping finance the monasteries and the surrounding towns and villages.

To this day the towns and villages along the main Camino Frances depend to a high degree on income from passing pilgrims.

The Holy Grail, the cup that was believed to have been used by Jesus during the Last Supper, was used by Joseph of Arimathea to collect the blood of Jesus on the Cross. It was kept in the monastery for many centuries for protection from Muslim invaders.

Unsurprisingly, the decline of the monastery began in the 14th century when the Aragonese King Martino V took the Holy Grail to his palace in Zaragoza. When the monks asked for it back, he tricked them with a replica.

For the monks at San Juan de la Pena, the loss of the Holy Grail must have been traumatic, setting the stage for gradual decay. After a fire destroyed much of the monastery in 1675, the Monasterio Nuevo, or new monastery, was built farther up the mountain.

There were several fires that destroyed much of the monastery complex in the 17th century. Decay came with infighting and power struggles. Grants and privileges from the king were reduced and at times completely stopped. Loss of focus and purpose set in, with vows being broken and poor leadership.

The relic is kept today in the Cathedral of Valencia, and it could well be that famous cup sought for centuries as one of Christianity's most precious artifacts.

Countless legends surround the whereabouts of the Holy Grail. What could be verified was only that the material of the cup in Valencia indeed originates from Roman times, around 100 A.D.

A replica of the cup can still be seen today, positioned on an altar in San Juan de la Pena, stimulating many an imaginative mind on the powers of the relic.

Believers have been obsessed throughout the centuries with relics like the Shroud of Turin, said to be remnants of the cloth in which the body of Jesus was wrapped after being taken down from the cross after the crucifixion.

Healing power, a revelation or a personal transformation is often linked to such a relic—one of the reasons why the pilgrimage to Santiago became so popular during medieval times.

Never underestimate the power of the mind, of thought and prayer on the manifestation of a wish or the materialization of a thing.

The search for the Holy Grail is symbolic for the search of the power within, and the true essence of self. For centuries we have been indoctrinated by religion on what has to be believed to attain salvation.

Medieval man, who lived constantly with the reality of an early death through disease, war or famine, was in mortal fear of eternal damnation in the fires of hell. To avoid this terrible fate, it was necessary to repent, to vow allegiance to the pope and church and to pay tithes.

Religion is a belief structure and doctrine designed by man. Terrible wars have been fought throughout the history of mankind over what doctrine is true or false. The consciousness of man is, thankfully, evolving. Religion or theology can at best show the path toward spiritual experience, which is always within rather than imposed externally.

Critics of independently-minded scripture and belief are no longer burned at the stake. We are at the threshold of a much better understanding of the workings and evolution of mind.

At present we are still stuck with a mindset divided between a rigid fundamentalism and a nihilistic, non-comital consumerism.

Experiential spirituality is felt by the heart. It is the understanding and deep connection with soul and that which is much greater than the narrow confinement of self. It is the connection of the within to the without and alignment of the above with the below.

Some people feel this connection when they hear a beautiful song, experience unconditional love from another being, look into the eyes of their beloved pet, or smell the fragrance of a flower. There is no recipe but the heart senses what is authentic and true.

The question arises: What is soul? There are many interpretations and the term can be misleading. For me it is that deep connection to the interconnectedness of all things, the inner guide and friend. It knows intuitively what is right and what is wrong.

In our digital world of information overload it is more difficult than ever to hear that inner voice of truth and authenticity.

In the political discourse where truth becomes a lie and a lie is propounded as truth, it has become very difficult for the untrained mind to discern between fact and delusion.

Thumbing through the day on a smart phone connects you to a globally-connected world but separates you from the preciousness of the moment and what the universe might be trying to tell you through the rustling of leaves in a tree, the call of a blackbird, the beauty of a sunset or a sudden precious thought.

When you find yourself becoming a victim of distraction, refocus and count your breath by consciously inhaling and exhaling. Feeling your body and your breath will instantly bring you back to the moment. It is a perfect barometer of where you are. Are you stressed out? Are you relaxed or is your mind chasing another monkey?

When walking the Camino there might be times when you will be walking alone and in loneliness for hours. For some, it can be unbearable to be alone for even a few minutes.

On the Camino you meet a disparate group of people. Some are earnest pilgrims, others merely hikers. I've met people who miss the magic of the moment, walking in beautiful natural surroundings with their senses locked to an electronic gadget.

Is it the fear that when walking alone in unknown territory that the sluice gates of suppressed emotions could be laid bare?

It can be a real test of faith to overcome those feelings of fear, melancholy and sadness over that which has gone and is no more. Transmuting those emotions opens the gateway to that inner friend, the higher self or soul.

It takes time and effort to discover the inner Holy Grail. What is called enlightenment by the Buddhists comes at best after years of training mind and body with meditation and spiritual practice.

The Camino is no fast track to a spiritual awakening. It will merely reflect during your walk where you are at this point in time and where you might have to intensify your training.

But like the walk itself, it is easier to take each step as it comes and to avoid being disheartened by focusing on how far you still might have to go.

The Essentials

- Discover your inner spirit and Holy Grail with time alone.
- Soul is your inner friend and guide.
- Guard the gateway to your soul from constant distraction.

- Find time daily to disconnect from social media and other digital distractions.
- Move out of your comfort zone to walk in unknown territory.

Chapter 8

The Shadow

The ancient teachers of Jewish mysticism and self-development never wavered in warning their students to be watchful of the shadow side of character, especially the farther they walked on the spiritual path.

It is part of the human condition that we are imperfect beings. The sages of old were very much aware of the lure of the shadow, when the ego is saying, "I'm done with my training. I've learned what I have to learn. I know intuitively what is right or wrong. You don't have to tell me anything—I know!"

Fairytales are filled with images of the hero fighting the dragon. In Greek mythology we have the sirens, or dangerous creatures, luring sailors to shipwreck on the rocky shores of their island with enchanting music and song.

The Bible has Jesus spending forty days in the desert confronting the devil (the shadow). Moses withdraws to Mount Sinai.

In Buddhism the Tibetan Milarepa returns to his cave after gathering firewood, finding dragons everywhere. His first thought is to chase them away but then he decides to teach them compassion and kindness. When he looks around again, they have disappeared.

In Zen one of the most widely known images is the monk taming the wild bull as a synonym of harnessing the inner demon and animal nature of the human being. The struggle in taming the bull is part of the process of harmonizing the shadow with the soul and evaluating the advancement on the spiritual path.

Walking the Camino is walking a spiritual path. According to legend ancient man followed the Milky Way when Europe was still linked to Africa at its narrowest point at the Strait of Gibraltar.

Scientists have found that 11 caves in northern Spain at the sites of Altamira, El Castillo and Tito Bustillo date back to at least 40,800 years. This makes them the oldest known cave art in Europe. Celtic priests probably used the routes for rituals. Many towns and villages along the Camino still bear testimony to the ancient traditions in culture and architecture.

You can feel the magic of the Camino mostly when you walk alone and tune your senses to the mysterious frequency of the path. It is almost as if you can feel the pulse of all those hundreds of thousands of pilgrims who have walked in centuries prior the same very path you are walking on.

Pilgrims tell stories of the shadows of the past that come to the fore when you walk alone in unknown territory. Emotions stemming from incidents many years ago suddenly surface. "I didn't know I still hated my ex-husband so much … I thought I had overcome the grief over my mother's death…I felt all that remorse again."

The emotional and physical challenges—also called "walking through the valley of death"—often surface after the first few days of the walk or when the pilgrim starts thinking, *I've come to grips with it now. It's easier than I had thought.* Not without reason is there a saying:

"Be humble or the path will humble you."

Walking is a meditation and every desirable and undesirable thought and emotion will surface. It is important to accept this as the way forward and part of the process of growing.

Roger was one of those people fighting himself and everyone else in the world. He was constantly whining and complaining about the Camino during our walk. His girlfriend had persuaded him to join her on the Camino, which he did after much persuasion. He would have preferred spending his vacation on some beach in the Mediterranean, and kept telling everyone that he would rather be elsewhere.

After some days everyone, including his girlfriend, was avoiding grumpy Roger. His feet were hurting and he had come on the Camino unprepared physically and emotionally. He was constantly making sarcastic remarks about religious artefacts and the pilgrimage in general.

"It's just a hike and I could darn well have chosen a lot of nicer places to go hiking," he complained.

He had a special ire against the Catholic church, mocking their rituals, the pope, the Virgin Mary and anything else he could think of.

Like most of the others I didn't particularly like Roger. I sensed that some of the more devout pilgrims were getting increasingly upset about his remarks. A tempestuous Italian in the group threatened to punch Roger the next time he opened his mouth.

Roger was teaching all of us to avoid falling into the trap of being too quick in labeling and judging people by the way they act. You never know where they are coming from and what they had to endure in their lives.

From his girlfriend we later learned that Roger had a particularly strict religious upbringing and spent traumatic childhood years in a Catholic boarding school. We could only guess what he had gone through, judging from his anger at the church and its representatives in general.

After some days Roger's feet had become so blistered that he could only complete his journey by bus. We met him two weeks later outside the Cathedral in Santiago. He seemed wonderfully cheerful in a positive sense. Gone were the anger and sarcasm. Something had happened that will remain his secret but had transformed his perspective of the "sacred."

The universe in many ways rewards the "enlightened spirit". But it is not a given and often, as the Jewish mystics, pointed out, at that point when the student makes the biggest strides he is also most in danger of falling prey to the ego and losing his humility and sense of gratitude.

Sometimes the reward comes with power, wealth and influence. Whether these tools are used for the betterment of all living things and the raising of collective consciousness depends on how far the character has truly progressed and is aware of the pitfalls of the shadow.

True character shows itself when man or woman is entrusted with influence and power over others. The trap comes when you feel yourself sitting on a golden throne of perceived invincibility and fame.

Some few famous film, sports and rock stars have realized that with fame comes responsibility. Too often many others lose connection to their soul and succumb to the demons of substance and alcohol abuse. We only have to scan the headlines of the yellow press to realize that fame and fortune do not necessarily coincide with happiness.

I am appalled at how leaders of South Africa's ruling African National Congress (ANC) sacrificed once-cherished ideals to wanton corruption and nepotism. I knew many of them personally when they were living in exile, sharing the vision of a democratic and non-racial future, while living modest lives. Once in power they were quick to adopt the same habits as the lords of apartheid they fought—especially their arrogance.

Disaster is predestined if a character who has not transmuted his shadow is handed too much money and power.

Many world leaders appear to be driven by narcissism and self-aggrandizement, taking humanity many steps backwards at a time when vision and sense of purpose are required to address the challenges of our time.

But it is too easy to blame these leaders for "our misery." They merely reflect what is happening with human consciousness at a deeper level.

These leaders did not just happen. Democracy is a fragile plant that needs to be nurtured and protected.

We are living in an age where the shadow side of humanity is fueled by social media. We need only peruse comments on Twitter or Facebook on any controversial issue that opens a Pandora's box of bile that people throw at those who are of a different opinion.

Sound science, research and historical facts are buried in an avalanche of fake news. We need to constantly stand guard at the doorway of our soul so that we are aware of the shadow.

Swiss psychiatrist Carl Gustav Jung wrote, "Unfortunately, there can be no doubt that man is, on the whole, less good than he imagines himself or wants himself to be. Everyone carries a shadow, and the less it is embodied in the individual's conscious life, the blacker and denser it is."

Typical for the shadow is when we transfer a perceived personal inferiority in ourselves onto someone else and view it as the other person's failing or problem.

Another person—typically marriage partner, family member, boss or colleague–could be a reflection of an unpleasant aspect of our own personality that has not been transformed.

What irritates us most about the actions of another person is often what most irritates us about ourselves.

Americans are asked whether they are Republican or Democrat. You are called upon to make a choice and whatever argument the other side brings forward will be rejected.

The pervasive divisiveness in society flashes to the surface on most race, gender, class, nationality, and religious issues.

Very often the anger originates from an old hurt that goes back generations in a family or a country's history. It can be pervasive in a whole country or society where the feelings of guilt, hurt and anger over racial exploitation or persecution of a minority have not been dealt with.

With neither side listening to the other or willing to engage in dialogue, there has grown an explosive powder keg, inflaming especially those mentally unstable personalities on the fringes of society.

In the confrontation with the opposite, identity and belief are defined. There is good and bad, black and white, rich and poor, Christian and Muslim. It is, however, merely a perspective. Reality is far more complex and in myriad colors and shades of grey.

This is why the yin and yang symbol from the Daoist/Taoist tradition is such a beautiful concept of two halves forming the whole. Neither yin or yang is absolute. Each contains the beginning aspect of the other in a constant flow like night turning into day and day turning into night. The female aspect also has male aspects and the male aspect something of the female.

Too much yin or too much yang in any system creates an imbalance, whether in nature, body functions, or economic or political structures.

We are all susceptible to burying parts of our character that we find unacceptable in the subconscious mind. The problem is that if we don't face the shadow aspect at the doorway to our mind, it becomes so big that it takes over.

The first step is acknowledging the shadow aspect by accepting that anger, malice, sadness or vindictiveness. A rule of thumb is that what upsets us the most in our fellow man has a connection to our own shadow.

We should ask the following questions:

What is it that annoys me most about what that person is doing?

Is that person mirroring aspects of my own self that I am not seeing?

Why am I having this reaction and what do I have to learn from this incident?

How can I recast the villain to be the teacher?

How can I avoid feeding the drama or being triggered by something the other person has done or said?

In cultivating self-love and self-compassion, the mantra could be:

"I am angry and upset, but I still love and accept myself the way I am."

You can practice self-compassion by pinpointing and writing down the shadow aspects of your character such as hatred or cowardice and replacing and transmuting them with the opposites such as love and courage.

The Essentials

- Accept the shadow aspects of your character. You are human and not perfect!
- Transmute the shadow aspects with the positives, e.g., compassion replaces anger, love replaces hate, focus replaces distraction.
- Cultivate self-love and self-compassion.
- With power and influence comes responsibility.
- Humility is the first step to self-recognition.

Chapter 9

Emotional Shifters

We are imperfect human beings and life is not always an easy ride. We have bad days where everything seemingly goes wrong.

You miss the first way marker out of town and get lost because you are grumpy. You were woken by loud pilgrims in the early hours of the morning. You avoided taking a shower because the bathroom was dirty and there was no hot water.

A chain reaction follows where you get to the next town late and find out that there is no accommodation. That means another five kilometer (3.10 mile) walk to the next town. The mood couldn't be worse.

Such days happen when you get locked into a negative downward spiral that attracts even more negativity.

How you feel when you arise in the morning and whether your dreams are predominantly positive or negative is very much a barometer of where you are at a subconscious level.

Self-reflection is crucial in such moments so that you remain in control and do not allow the events of the day to drive you into a downward spiral.

The inability to look at the demons inside, coupled with the lack of self-esteem and self-love, is a major reason you fall prey to the countless distractions competing for your attention.

You think you will be happy and all your problems will be solved when you move to a different town, change jobs, get a new partner and a new car–forgetting that you are always taking yourself with you.

Beneath the urge in venting negative emotions are the cemented feelings not allowed to surface. These feelings could be an old hurt, anger and fear. It is deep spiritual work to look at the shadow.

Alone time, time for solitude and self-reflection, is crucial to getting to know yourself and your feelings. How can you transmute those feelings of depression anger and resentfulness into positive vibrations?

Part of the problem of the human mind is that we have learned through evolution to focus on the negative. It's part of our survival DNA. This is why mass media focuses on negative news nearly all the time. The mass media is merely fulfilling a human desire that pulls our focus away from the good things that are happening at the same time.

Our adrenaline shoots up each time we hear about some major accident or natural catastrophe. Our hunter and gatherer ancestors learned to read weather patterns and studied the geography of their environment in order to survive.

Stress hormones have an important function in alerting our fight or flight hormones. Our blood pressure goes up, our heart starts racing and our muscles tense up. The phenomenon is patently visible in those nature documentaries where a pack of lions attacks a herd of antelope. There is mad panic until the moment when one of the antelopes gets killed. The herd almost immediately calms down and very often they can be seen resuming their grazing while the lions are still eating.

We modern humans have to re-program ourselves to this natural sprint and recovery system.

In our modern age the countless digital distractions, stressful jobs, fast food nutrition, lack of exercise and negative emotions keep our stress hormones at an unhealthy, almost constantly high level.

If you don't have a rest-and-recovery system in place the body is in a constant state of alert, using a lot of vital nutrients and energy. Vital organs will not be functioning as they should be and the result is a general feeling of fatigue and listlessness.

It is no surprise that mental illnesses and burnout are fast reaching epidemic proportions in the Western world.

We first and foremost need regular time-out sessions. Such a time-out session is a time of the day where you go completely offline from all those emails and social media sites.

Nobody can possibly be a top performer by spending ten or sixteen hours in the office. The world's most successful entrepreneurs spend surprisingly little time at "work." What they have learned is very effective time management and delegating tasks to the right people.

Companies with a worryingly high rate of absenteeism often have a work ethic that results in high stress for all. Employees are afraid to take their breaks and when they do, they have their lunch at the place of work, multi-tasking on the telephone or PC. Sometimes they are even afraid to take vacation time. You are expected to put in more hours than in your work contract but nobody appears to ask how effective that work really is.

After hitting a wall in my previous career in a large media organization and on the verge of a burnout, I decided to walk the Camino the first time in 2007.

I walked a small section but this "first retreat" got me hooked. Today I am fortunate enough to be able to take a personal retreat of two to three weeks every year, and I have done most of them on the Camino.

You can only effectively practice emotional shifting when you are aligned. One of the best ways of realignment is focusing the mind on your breathing. The Vietnamese monk Thich Nath Hanh has developed some wonderful breathing exercises:

Breathing in, I calm my body.

Breathing out, I smile.

Dwelling in the present moment, I know this is a wonderful moment.

(Hanh, Thich Nhat. *Living Buddha, Living Christ* (p. 16). Ebury Publishing. Kindle Edition.)

Breathing in, I am fully aware that I am breathing in.

Breathing out, I am fully aware that I am breathing out.

It is best when you practice such breathing standing up with your feet grounded on the floor. Your chin is bent slightly downward to your breastbone so that your neck muscles are slightly stretched. The focal point on the top of your head is aligned with an imaginary point 60 cm above the head.

When you are sitting, you will not be aligned and your breathing becomes forced from the upper part of your body (stress posture) and not from your relaxed lower belly.

A good indicator of relaxed breathing is when you can barely hear your own inhaling and exhaling.

You can also apply slow meditative walking.

Breathing in, I take a step. Breathing out, I take a step.

At this point you can start looking at some imaginary emotional shifters that can instantly change your mood. One idea is to keep a collection of special pictures on your smart phone where you know that they will lift your mood–that favorite spot on your last vacation, the picture of a loved one, a funny video that will make you laugh.

Most importantly, what are my three greatest gifts? What gratitude moments or joyful moments did I have during the past 24 hours? It is not only important to look at these images but to relive them with your feelings. Where in my body do I feel again that "happy moment?"

After only three or four minutes practicing such a ritual you will feel your energy expanding to a positively higher level.

Be kind: It's a no-brainer. Being kind, smiling and friendly to others will naturally draw kind people into your energy sphere.

It costs absolutely nothing to show courtesy and politeness in attitude and behavior to others in public. Some political leaders have unfortunately set very bad examples on this in the recent past.

The degeneration into bad behavior and derogatory language has become the norm in much of the extremely polarized political discourse. It sets a tone.

Your vocabulary will show where you are at and whether you are mindful with your words.

Words and sound have a vibrational energy that affects your body positively or negatively. Research conducted on 700 million words and phrases used on Facebook by the University of Warwick, United Kingdom, in 2013 revealed some astonishing facts.

Neurotic people disproportionately used the phrase 'sick of' and the word 'depressed'. Research conducted by Eichstaedt et al. in 2015 found a correlation between language used on Twitter accounts and heart disease in U.S. counties where words expressing anger, hate and resentment were predominantly used.

Healing words, especially those expressing gratitude and love, have a healing effect, as the Japanese researcher Dr. Masaru Emoto showed in his experiments on water crystals (www.masaru-emoto.net).

I have seen several pilgrims on the Camino humming prayers and mantras while walking.

The old languages of Sanskrit, Aramaic and Latin are particularly powerful in their vibrational healing energy and cleansing the mind of negative thoughts and emotions.

The mantra **om mani padme hum** is the practicing of a path of indivisible union of method and wisdom, transforming impure body, speech and mind into the pure exalted body, speech and mind of the Buddha.

The Lord's Prayer in Aramaic, the language spoken by Jesus, is one of my favorites. It starts with **"Abwoon D'bashmaya."** It is a rendition

"Our Father in Heaven," which in the original Aramaic is more closely translated as: "Source of Being that manifests all things."

Concentrating on mantras and breathing exercises is a valuable exercise in thought control. Some of the most successful people in history had very good control of their thoughts. Albert Einstein was rumored to have practiced gratitude each day to all the great scientists who had lived before him.

South Africa's Nelson Mandela, who was imprisoned for 27 years by the apartheid regime, every day visualized his dream of one day becoming president of a democratically-ruled rainbow nation.

Thought control, coupled with persistence, is a hallmark of all great leaders.

A common thread in the teachings of the great sages is the ability to practice self-control in regulating one's emotions, thoughts and behavior as a means of avoiding pain and suffering. It is one of the easiest and yet hardest things to do. In the age of social media and political demagogues "the right to vent" has become the norm.

A single uncontrolled outburst of anger has so often ruined a long-term relationship, destroyed a team or scuttled a potentially lucrative business deal.

We are living in an age where the shadow side of humanity is fueled by social media. Sound science, research and historical facts are buried in an avalanche of fake news. More than ever it has become a real challenge to stand guard at the gateway to the soul when it comes to avoiding the avalanche of junk information around us.

What subtle influence are you allowing to enter your mind? Is it predominantly negative or positive? What people are you surrounding yourself with? Are they allowed to enter your room? Are these people uplifting you or pulling you down in their own negative spiral?

Who are the five most important, uplifting, wonderful people you would be willing to spend time with on a lonely island?

How have you structured your immediate environment? Is your backpack, your room, your office cluttered with old stuff? Is it in harmony and beauty with your true self?

The Essentials

- Alone time is crucial for self-reflection.
- Your first feeling after waking up in the morning is a barometer of your subconscious mind.
- Blocked toxic feelings cause stress and harm the immune system.
- Language has energy. Be mindful of your vocabulary.
- Surround yourself with uplifting people and an uplifting environment.
- Concentrate on relaxed breathing when walking.
- Learn a healing mantra or prayer.

Chapter 10

Asking for Help

Walking unprepared without checking the weather situation, I once got hopelessly lost during a storm in the Pyrenees Mountains.

The worst of my fears was dying slowly of exposure in subzero temperatures. Normally, walking most hiking trails in western Europe, you inevitably run across people who are only too willing to help you find the right path.

After hours of walking on the remote mountain track, I had still not met a single human being and I could hear thunder in the distance. All sorts of horror scenarios started bouncing in my head.

Weather in the mountains can change by the hour, especially in the Pyrenees. Year after year hikers get lost and die of exposure when having to spend the night in freezing temperatures, dressed only in light summer hiking clothing.

When desperate there is only one way out. Ask the universe for help. I was lucky to find shelter beneath a rocky outcrop where I could wait for the storm to pass.

Then I just kept walking to keep myself warm.

Eventually, through an opening in dense undergrowth I saw a glimmer of light that led me to a remote village and a warm place to stay.

We get lost in many more ways than losing our way on a hike. Impermanence is a hallmark of life. Marriages break up. We lose our job. We lose our mobility and physical strength because of an illness or old age.

The sadness over that which has been lost or is no more can be extremely debilitating. Out of a false pride we refuse to ask for help when we hit the ground or are afraid we might be rejected by those persons we might want to go to for help.

The truth is that most people are only too happy to help when asked.

For every grumpy and bad-tempered grouse there are at least 100 other people who are kind and thoughtful.

I have been on remote paths of the Camino without any way markers or electronic gadgets to find my way. I had to ask the first person around for directions. I have had some of the most wonderful meetings with total strangers, who accompanied me for part of the way or struck up conversations in a Spanish I did not understand.

Not asking for help because we fear being rejected is embedded in our genes. We humans are programmed to live in family and community. It was part of our survival strategy in ancient times. We were dependent on each other for support in daunting environmental conditions.

Being pushed out of the warm cave because of bad behavior almost certainly was a death sentence in ancient times. We therefore tend to want to please others more than we need to and especially not to be a nuisance.

I met a woman on the Camino who had a backpack that was obviously too heavy for her. As a result, she was having problems with her knees and back. It took her a huge amount of courage to ask the hostel to have her backpack sent by taxi to the next town.

"I have such a guilty conscience," she confided to me. "It's like cheating."

I told her that there was nobody except herself who had this idea that going on a lengthy pilgrimage walk had to mean suffering–like she was undergoing some sort of crucifixion.

She looked a little relieved but I could see she still had that little nagging feeling inside.

God, or the Universe, whatever you might call the higher intelligence, has not meant us to suffer. Mostly we are the cause of our own suffering.

If circumstances or bad decisions force us into an untenable situation we can ask for help in prayer. And God sometimes sends us angels in the form of humans to help us just at the moment when we really need it.

Sometimes people simply have to say "no" for countless reasons and not because they don't like you.

It was something I really had to learn in the early stages of my health consultancy business. I had no customers and zero income. My financial reserves were fast depleting.

People had advised me that I should under no circumstances try to get my business up and running with cold calls. After spending a lot of money on advertising, I did it anyway and out of pure necessity.

Yes, I've had many rejections. But I also won some of my best premium customers after an initial cold call contact. What I had to learn was that if I did nothing I was going to lose anyway. By cold calling potential customers, I could only win.

If you are courteous and friendly, the other person will inevitably also be so. Sometimes the time or the product is just not suitable and you don't have to feel personally offended if you get a "no" for an answer.

Getting a rejection, the initial feeling is that of "being excluded" from the cave. But you have to understand where that feeling is coming from. Is it a hurt ego, not feeling worthy or confident enough? Are you really authentic in selling a product or don't you believe in it yourself and just want to make a quick buck? Most importantly: Have you communicated enough the benefit the other person would receive from buying your product or service?

You are like most people, who simply have a good feeling inside when they give unconditionally and don't expect anything in return.

We live in a culture where we immediately expect something back from the person we assisted. I've been in situations where I got the least appreciation from the people I perceived to have helped more than any others. But the universe doesn't work that way.

When we help unconditionally and without reward the universe does always give back. It seldom comes back from the same person but in some other way you least expect and at a time and place you least expect.

We get the most from life by giving the most and helping the most. Yet we constantly seek validation from the people we like the least through external beauty, position and possession, which are all temporary.

The burning desire to be validated, to be admired and to be appreciated often comes from a feeling of insecurity and deprivation. That feeling, however, can only be overcome when we give and we help out of a feeling of abundance and prosperity.

The Essentials:

- Don't know a way out? There are always people who can and are only too willing to help.
- Not asking is losing. When asking you might lose but you can also win.
- Giving unconditionally without expecting anything in return gives a good feeling.
- Desire to be validated and admired comes from insecurity and deprivation.

Chapter 11

The Authentic Body Mind

Your body is the most authentic recording device of everything that has happened in your life. You will dream of events that happened decades ago because those memories are stored away somewhere in the depths of your body cells.

When you dream of when you were a seven-year-old and stole the cookies from Grandma's closet, you have in some way not closed with that incident emotionally.

Your head-mind probably made up all sorts of reasons why taking those cookies was in order, while your sub-conscious heart-mind knew very well that what you did was stealing and that you hurt Grandma because you lied to her.

A tension or dissonance between head-mind and heart-mind, like acting against a gut feeling or doing something where all the alarm bells are running at a heart level, are just those things that the body will always remember.

Training your "heart-mind" to be emotionally mature is one of the reasons we are here on earth. We humans are imperfect beings, and probably the most disconnected of species from ourselves and our natural environment.

We have incarnated as souls to use our bodies as instruments of learning.

The heart is not merely an organ of the cardiovascular system that transports nutrients, oxygen and hormones throughout the body and removes metabolic waste. In the spiritual sense the heart is described as the "seat of the soul." It is the first organ that develops in the fetus and is the connection between our physical and non-physical (soul) selves.

Impulses or thoughts flow first from the heart and then to the brain. The brain dissects, rationalizes and analyzes. The "heart-mind" is authentic and closest to the true self or soul purpose. Knowing the difference between "head-mind" and "heart-mind" is the spiritual learning part.

Our body is constantly sending us signals about what we need to hear and work on. The problem is that we are so caught up in the world of distraction that we mostly fail to listen until the body gets really angry and calls a time-out with some illness or malady. It is no surprise that cardiovascular diseases top the list in much of the Western world.

Regaining that connection to the "heart-mind" comes mostly during times of solitude, during meditation, prayer and deep walking. That is when we become aware of our emotional state of being. Some of the "emotional memories" stored in the body could go back many years or even decades.

These energies can be transmuted very well with the ancient body arts of tai chi, qi gong and yoga that were all developed and refined by spiritual masters over many generations.

It is only fairly recent that these ancient arts have reached the Western world. One of the great tai chi masters, Cheng Mang Ching, was ostracized by the Chinese community in New York when he began teaching tai chi for the first time to Western students in the early 1960s.

If you walk the main Camino Frances, you will be walking for five weeks or longer. After two or three weeks on the road you realize that the Camino is much more than a mere physical exercise.

Not only does the body start detoxing, but I have noticed on my walks that dreams, childhood events, and memories of traumatic relationships that occurred many years ago return with a particular clarity.

These are particularly precious healing moments when old trauma is released to open up the channels for a flow of new energy.

Whatever the heart-mind hasn't transmuted emotionally will at some stage come back to haunt you. It is why the mother on her death bed has that last wish before dying to reconcile with the son she hasn't spoken to for years.

Volunteers and therapists companioning the dying have told me that the deepest regret is most often not having made amends with innermost family members. A peaceful death then only comes when that "something" has been dealt with.

What Chinese medicine has known for centuries, modern medicine is confirming with latest research. Many a serious illness has its origins in emotional baggage stored in the body-mind.

There is a particularly poignant passage in the third Beatitude of the Bible: "Blessed are the meek, for they shall inherit the earth."

In the original Aramaic language, spoken by Jesus, the meaning is more subtle: "Tubwehun l' makiche d'hinnon nertun arha." This roughly translates to: "Renewal to those in emotional turmoil and blessed are those who can soften that which has hardened in their bodies."

While walking in solitude you will inevitably be confronted by the same phenomenon as when lying alone awake at night: Hundreds of thoughts will be passing through your mind of past and future things.

One thought chases the next as you wind yourself up and down in a spiral of dancing monkeys in the head.

You won't control those thoughts by practicing mind control methods. The mind does become aware of what it is thinking about and can extract itself with an accusatory finger of "why can't I think of something else? Why can't I let go of these worrying concerns in my head?"

You will notice that as the body releases tension during your walk, those dancing monkeys gradually start disappearing as you begin the descent from the head into feeling the body.

This is best done by aligning to the present moment by focusing on your breathing and counting the inhaling and exhaling of breaths.

You can also start by feeling each step touching the ground, feeling the ground and how the energy of the earth moves from your foot up your legs, spinal cord, neck and the crown of your head. Start by walking very slowly, aware of the present moment, just concentrating on these small things to liberate your mind.

Our ancestors practiced ceremony and rituals to transmute trauma on a body level. Animals still have this mechanism intact. A herd of antelope will run apparently haphazardly in all directions when one of them has been killed by a predator. Their bodies shiver and shake, but minutes later all has passed and they will resume grazing as if nothing has happened.

Dogs have much to deal with as companions of us "difficult humans." After experiencing a stressful situation dogs will sometimes go into turbo-mode, running helter-skelter around the house. It is nothing more than the releasing of energy.

I don't recommend humans go "zooming" around the house but we do need to rediscover some of our own ancient rituals for dealing with trauma.

The Zulu people I grew up with in South Africa's KwaZulu Natal province on occasions had all-night ecstatic dancing and drumming sessions.

As a young boy I remember being deeply moved by a group of male inmates of a local prison digging a trench by the roadside with a grim-faced white warden standing guard next to them, his hand close to the belt holding his revolver.

Their singing found a natural pitch and rhythm with the swinging of shovels hitting the ground. It was their way of dealing with the hard labor in the midday heat and the many other terrible abuses common in prisons of apartheid South Africa at the time.

In the rural areas during my childhood it was still quite common to hear the drums and the wonderful singing from the African villages echoing through the valleys.

These voices and sounds sadly receded as South Africa became increasingly urbanized, and thousands of black villages were forcibly moved to distant homelands by the apartheid regime, causing people to lose connection to their roots that were deeply embedded in the soils where their ancestors lie buried.

Spain had to deal with its own trauma during the fascist Franco dictatorship that lasted until the early 1970s. But much of the ancestral spirit can still be found in the rural areas.

In the Galician section of the Camino, it is not uncommon to walk into a village to find the locals enjoying a colorful festival of dancing and singing. Many of the rituals can be traced back to early Celtic times, very similar to the Irish folk dances still popular today.

Some of the religious rituals and processions I have seen on the Camino obviously seem to have taken much of their cues from the pre-Christian era.

While observing and participating in all-night village festivities, I have often wondered where we lost connection with our ancestors. The history of our past is embedded in our genes and all the ancient cultures honor that heritage with great respect, knowing how important this aspect is for the mental health of a community.

Walking the ancient pilgrimage paths of Europe reconnects both on a personal and much deeper level.

In medieval times it was common for one member of the family to walk the Camino to cleanse the past wrongs that had been committed in the family system.

A ritual that is regaining popularity is the placing of stones on the way markers with the scallop shell: One stone is placed for each member of the family going down the male and female lineage.

I have placed stones for family members and especially friends going through a rough time. Very often they came back to me, noticing a change only days after the Camino ritual.

There are many deeper aspects of the Camino that will remain a mystery. I would go along with researcher and author Rupert Sheldrake's theory of "morphic resonance."

Sheldrake's hypothesis has led to a radically new interpretation of memory storage in the brain and of biological inheritance.

Thus, every member of a species inherits a collective memory from past members, contributing to the collective memory and affecting other members of the species in the future.

The family constellation therapy system developed by Bernd Hellinger, and drawing much from the Zulu tradition, advances the theory that past trauma often comes from unresolved issues or unspoken truths in the family past.

The fact that my father was driven into a nervous breakdown by my authoritarian grandfather's high expectations was never spoken about, but only came into the open during a constellation of my own family system.

I have personally witnessed a constellation where a woman living in Germany had been suffering for years because her father had suddenly left the family when she was a young girl. Only some days after the matter was resolved in a family constellation, her father, living in the United States, called for the first time in years.

The "morphic resonance" of the prayers, rituals and personal trials of the many pilgrims who have gone before on the Camino over the centuries can certainly be felt.

I strongly believe that there are places on earth with a strong energy frequency, the Camino being part of a powerful earth meridian system—a matrix of connective pathways resembling the human circulatory, nervous, or acupuncture meridian systems.

The main energy vortexes, chakras or acupuncture points would thus include such powerful places as the pyramids of Giza in Egypt, the Temple Mount in Jerusalem, the Cathedral of Santiago de Compostela, Lourdes, Stonehenge, the Mayan temple locations and the Easter Island heads in Polynesia–places millions of people seem to be naturally drawn to.

One of the great tragedies of mankind is his disconnect from himself and thus his treatment of the environment. The Camino is one of the few remaining ancient paths of ritual, although much has been lost to the modern highways now crossing the Iberian peninsula.

Walking anywhere, be it in the beautiful parks of London or New York, will of course always be good for your health and mental well-being. But walking the ancient paths of pilgrimage will reconnect you to an even deeper, spiritual level, if you open your senses to the magic around you.

The Essentials
- Your body is the most authentic feedback mechanism.
- Reconnecting with your body heals unresolved trauma.
- Rituals reconnect body, mind and soul.
- Find alone time and solitude to reconnect with the heart-mind.
- Time spent in nature is healing.

Chapter 12
Embrace Your Self

Walking alone and going into introspection on the Camino is as interesting as watching fellow pilgrims on the Way.

A fairly sizeable number of folk approach the Camino as a means of physical exercise, racing on a bicycle to get to the next town as fast as possible or speeding past you with flailing walking sticks in a half-walking, half-running pace.

I would call this the hurried "treadmill approach," not very different from the fast-paced life at home. If you are on a bicycle you would also have to travel many of the routes on tarmac, missing out on some of the most scenic spots that are only accessible by foot.

In recent years tour operators have been taking busloads of day tourists to walk small sections of the last 100 kilometer (62 miles) stretch of the Camino between the town of Sarria and Santiago de Compostela. The noisy chatter of the maddening crowds, the huge amounts of trash left by the wayside, and way markers defaced by graffiti is a far cry from the Camino spirit on the lonelier and more rugged pathways farther north.

This is where you experience the real magic of nature, hearing the gentle munching of the cows on the meadows and observing the birds of prey circling the sky above the majestic mountains of the Camino Primitivo.

Animals are totally connected to their immediate environment, sniffing, smelling and using all their senses to imbibe the immediate moment, with no past or future.

Much of the Western mind seems to have lost its soul in the mad rush for immediate gratification and the addiction to external approval in its many variations.

It has become very difficult to discern who we really are on a soul-purpose level when we are bombarded by a pop culture from the moment we get up in the morning and take that stretch toward the smart phone.

In contrast to the true self, the false forces want to make us believe in self-images, or "false Gods," with a manipulative purpose. Many of the rich and famous "role models" on glitzy magazine covers show exceedingly dysfunctional behavior. Some are obviously very unhappy people.

A growing number of neuroscientists even believe that we are a species with no free will and can be manipulated in any direction if the communicator knows how to play the reptilian part of the brain–the oldest part of the brain–with strong emotions such as anger and fear.

The historian and author of the book *Sapiens—A brief history of humankind*, Yuval Noah Harari, said recently that he is most concerned that "we are close to the point when an external system can understand your feelings better than you. We've already seen a glimpse of it in the last epidemic of fake news."

Knowing and embracing your true self can thus become a matter of survival. If we don't live our true self, we can become very unhappy and fall ill, because the body is always reflecting what is happening in the mind.

We need only to look at the skyrocketing figures for depression and substance abuse in the Western world to realize that something is seriously out of sync.

The tragedy is that some of the most effective means of human self-development and the raising of consciousness are very simple and free. The catch is that the simple and easy is also the most difficult to follow through.

Finding and embracing yourself is pretty easy if you take time out for introspection. This can be anything: time for prayer, meditation, pilgrimage walks, body-mind retreats and other methods that bring us back into alignment with the higher or true self. We need to learn again who we really are.

Liberating yourself from the powers of distraction that alienate you from your true self is the real challenge of our time.

Each one of us alive today has a spark of the divine, has desire and purpose, unique abilities and something precious to give back. It will for the most part not be as a "YouTube influencer" or other image that fits the pop culture's definition of success.

We have the choice when we wake up to each new day to choose the high road of our higher destiny or the low road.

In the religious sense we would speak of what God expects of us as a co-creator to a higher plane of evolution and becoming the best expression of ourselves.

But we live in a polarized world. There is the other side, or what religion calls Satan—those dark forces that pull us back to the low road.

So let us look at some of the differences between the true and the false self.

The true or divine self is closely aligned with soul purpose, or why you are here on earth. The soul, or divine spark, is aligned with God or the universe. It is a giving, serving energy for the betterment of all living beings.

Martin Luther King was quoted as saying that "not everybody can be famous but everyone can be great and greatness is determined by service."

We intuitively feel when we are walking the right path. It is when everything falls into place and seems to flow naturally. Our walk is easy and without strain or effort. We feel our heart opening and the energy level rising in mind and body. We have a joyful stride and feel at one with the universe. These are the moments of contentment and happiness.

The higher plane of serving consciousness takes only a short time to transmute the lower energies that come with humiliation, rejection, anger and fear.

It is a giving instead of a taking energy. It is unitary instead of divisive: the unconditional love of the mother holding the child in her arms, helping without expecting anything in return because you know its just right, just being kind and gracious.

We recognize those people on a higher plane of consciousness instantly when they enter and move a room—a wave of positive energy spreads itself into the hearts of people.

I had one such particularly moving experience in 1990 when I was lucky enough to meet Nelson Mandela with a small group of reporters, some months after his release from prison. It was immediately apparent to me that here was a man with higher thought and vision.

Mandela had every reason to fan the flames of hate toward the white Afrikaners who had incarcerated him but instead spread the message of hope, forgiveness and reconciliation. What a contrast to the picture we were indoctrinated with as children growing up in South Africa—that of a dangerous terrorist.

Many years later I had a similar experience at an event in Hamburg, Germany, with the Dalai Lama. The Tibetan leader has every reason to hate the Chinese for destroying his homeland and persecuting the Tibetan Buddhists. Instead, he spoke of forgiveness and absorbing the energy of hate with love as a necessary precondition to end the cycle of suffering.

How often in history have we seen the persecuted becoming the persecutors in an endless cycle of hate and retribution, my country South

Africa being a particular case in point? The white Afrikaners were them-selves victims of British imperialism in the Anglo-Boer War when hun-dreds of thousands of women and children died from disease and illness in concentration camps.

The greatest leaders of our time have understood this crucial mes-sage. It is why the fathers of the European Union did not go the same way as their predecessors after World War I in punishing and humiliating Germany. The result: Central Europe has experienced the longest era of peace and prosperity in its history.

But we always need to be wary of the shadow lurking in the back-ground. We are imperfect humans and will fall prey to its tentacles again and again. Typically, when we are in the shadow our mood and energy are at much lower levels. This is running with the ranting crowd.

The lower self is ego-driven and centered around external approval, self-aggrandizement and immediate gratification. Much of our culture is dominated by the shadow.

When you are not clear and aligned with your key values, you will always get caught in the tentacles of the shadow. The questions that need to be asked, basically with everything that comes our way, are: Is this serving my higher purpose and destiny? Does this comply with my value system? Does this increase or decrease my energy?

- We become the people we associate ourselves the most with. Do the five people you spend most time with emanate a positive or a negative energy?
- Any type of substance abuse or addiction will catapult you into a downward spiral of poor physical and mental health.
- What type of information are you feeding your mind? Most mass media outlets will bombard you with negative news. How about funny movies to lift your energy!
- What foods are you eating? Junk food, especially processed foods and sodas, will not only make you fat but lower your mental thought capacity and drive.

- Lack of body movement and exercise has a major influence on our body metabolism and mood. Our body is made to walk at least 20 kilometers a day. Most people who work in an office today don't manage a fraction of that.

The rate of mental breakdown and burnout has reached epidemic proportions. During my years of consulting in corporate health, we found that a lot of people out there are exceedingly unhappy in the jobs they are doing.

If you are forced to perform tasks or get stuck in a niche where you are doing things that contradict your personal calling and value system, your very soul nature will start hurting and going into rebellion.

Often this comes about due to bad organizational structure and leadership: The social worker or doctor spends a good part of the day with bureaucracy instead of helping people face-to-face. Selling a product that you know is harmful to other people and the environment. The company you are working for is involved in unethical practices and work methods. A growing number of employees are forced into globally standardized work procedures, with little or no freedom to express individual talent or ideas. Authoritarian leadership structures dominate the business.

Embracing your true self and staying true to your calling will at times require exceptional courage to make the required changes. It could mean leaving a well-paid but unsatisfying job. It could mean leaving a long but dysfunctional and energy-draining relationship. It is taking the more difficult road, the road of uncertainty, where you might get lost initially and have to overcome all sorts of obstacles—most of them probably coming from immediate family and friends.

"You can't do that. You are risking everything! You will never make it. You will land under the bridge."

Be assured that if you stay true to your call, the universe will always reward you at the right time and place, in more ways than you can imagine possible.

The Essentials:

- Be totally true to your core values.
- Look at every major decision and action in terms of your personal values.
- Soul purpose is in flow, non-divisive and of a serving energy. It is the universal energy creating through you on a higher plane of consciousness.
- Embracing yourself is embracing the divine energy within you.

Chapter 13

Walking Alone

The ancient masters of all the great religions recommended time alone as a crucial means of discovering your true self.

Jesus took 40 days for time alone in the desert to confront his own shadow and the demons of temptation. Moses removed himself alone to Mount Sinai to receive the Ten Commandments from God.

It is in the time spent alone that we come closest to the divine and our life purpose.

In walking the Camino, the temptation is great to walk together with the wonderful people you meet along the way.

There is a natural bonding in sharing the trials and tribulations of dealing with blisters, bad weather, getting lost or sharing a crowded hostel room with others.

The sharing of the emotional rollercoaster that comes with walking the path is a precious part of the experience of a walk lasting several weeks.

I have been on the Camino almost completely alone for several days. I have walked it with a good friend, with my wife, with a group that I guided and with people I met by chance along the way.

The worst and best experience was the time alone. Pilgrims mostly understand very well when a person they are walking with falls silent and needs time alone.

It is what the Chinese philosophers called the empty space between the spokes of the wheel that is more important than the spoke itself.

It is in that empty, dark space between the stars where you touch the divine.

I am convinced that the constant distractions with which the Western mind is confronted is one of the root causes of unhappiness and depression.

We as a society are obsessed with what the wise ancients called the distractions of the 10,000 things.

The news media feed on negative news; the constant subliminal messages working our emotions instill a need for material things we mostly don't need. There is confusion between necessity and want.

Lifestyles of the rich and famous are propagated in the yellow press and serve as role models that have very little relevance to reality.

It is no coincidence that with the addiction to distraction there are very few people who can truly bear to spend time alone.

We are also social animals and need constant interaction with our fellow human beings to feel safe.

It is ingrained in our genes because our ancestors were hunter and gatherer communities that depended on each other's support and help. A

person who was excluded from the tribe for a serious transgression inevitably faced certain death.

We are thus constantly seeking the accolades through social media as a reassurance. But they will seldom lead you onto the path of deeper spiritual experience.

It is during the walk alone, the time-out during a silent retreat and the alone time in nature where the gateway to the soul opens and you begin to realize who you truly are.

It is during the alone time that we discover the heart, the love and the divine within. It is who we truly are and that which the soul wants to illuminate.

Nelson Mandela found solace in the poem *Invictus* by William Ernest Henley.

Out of the night that covers me,
Black as the pit from pole to pole,
I thank whatever gods may be
For my unconquerable soul.
In the fell clutch of circumstance
I have not winced nor cried aloud.
Under the bludgeonings of chance
My head is bloody, but unbowed.
Beyond this place of wrath and tears
Looms but the Horror of the shade,
And yet the menace of the years
Finds and shall find me unafraid.
It matters not how strait the gate,
How charged with punishments the scroll,
I am the master of my fate,
I am the captain of my soul.

The poem is a rallying cry for all who dig deep into the self during those trying and desperate moments where there is seemingly no way out.

It is in the dark night of the soul, when we are humbled, humiliated, lying flat on the ground in desperation, rejection, fear and feeling lost in the dark pit of hopelessness, that we very often have the deepest spiritual experience.

When we experience the darkness of nights in the sadness, the fear and the melancholy, the first impulse is to want it to go away and to have it fixed.

But it is in the acceptance of this as being part of the human condition, the walking in the darkness of night that forces us to dig deep into our inner resources.

A crisis that can manifest itself in sadness, anger, irritation fear and all the other toxic emotions will in the end force us to take the necessary step forward.

The unconquerable soul is a gift from God, when the head can still be held high in surviving against all the odds. It is often when we know no way out that a door opens.

We all have our story of lying flat on the ground and knowing no way out and not knowing where to go next.

Tax authorities some years ago almost closed my consultancy business with a huge back payment demand, just after it turned its first year of profit.

Every time I was saved by "angels" in the human form whom I met just at the right time or who were sent at just the right time.

The universal message of *Invictus* is never to lose faith in the power of the soul. Even in the darkest of hours there is that first bright glimmer of hope.

We alone are in control of our thoughts and have nothing to fear but our own negative thoughts.

And these thoughts of the shadow inevitably come when we walk alone. It is useless to push them away. You go into negative self-talk. You are angry, sad, hurt, envious, narcissistic, hateful, and resentful.

When you accept the shadow of self you develop the ability to look also at the light, the beauty and the divine within.

It is the simple things, like a walk in nature, that will make you feel alive by getting into contact with your senses. You realize that you have higher qualities long buried under the mantle of self-doubt and self-rejection.

We are both light and shadow and only when we accept the truth of our shadow aspects can we look deeper and see the light of self-love.

The mantra is quite simple that can also be used very effectively in Emotional Freedom Tapping Techniques (EFT) by tapping certain acupuncture points while you are walking alone.

The first stage of the exercise is accepting the state of mind, such as *"I am sad, upset and angry."*

(Begin by tapping the karate chop point of your left hand, reciting the emotion you currently feel at least three times.

You then move to the next step by reciting the words: *I nevertheless fully love and accept myself the way I am.*

Saying the positive words, you then move down the body in this descending order:

✓ tapping both eyebrows
✓ the sides of the eye where the eyebrows end
✓ under the eye, directly under the pupil
✓ under the nose
✓ chin
✓ beginning of the collarbone
✓ under the left armpit
✓ at the top of the head point.

The Essentials:

• Walk alone.
• Carve out your alone time every day.
• In the darkest of nights the light often shines the brightest.
• Accept who you are. Love yourself with all that you are as a human—both the light and the shadow.

Chapter 14

Go Slow

One of the many lessons learned on a long walk is that you have to go slow to get far. If you walk too much on the first day of your hike, you will risk getting blisters and suffer from other physical ailments.

It's a fascinating phenomenon to watch on the Camino: A group of hikers will inevitably rise in the early hours of the morning to make tracks in order to stand first in line when the hostels at the next destination open. All the haste comes out of the fear of not finding a place to sleep.

In some of the remote towns hostels for pilgrims are indeed rare. But on all my many walks on the Camino, I have always found a place to stay.

The Spanish people are incredibly hospitable and friendly toward pilgrims walking the Camino. If worst comes to worst a sports hall or school classroom is opened with mattresses on the floor. Villagers in the towns have even been seen offering their private bedrooms to tired pilgrims.

The Camino is in many ways an analogy of life and you inevitably take yourself with you on a journey. It is obvious that many pilgrims take a time-out from their stressed-out lives at home and have difficulty switching to a calm, slowed-down rhythm.

In the revved-up treadmill of life in our modern cities, people are constantly in a hurry to get someplace. The preoccupied mind is buzzing with all the distractions thrown at it. You will find very few people walking mindfully slow at airports or bus stations. I've done the experiment of deliberately slowing my walk and have found people pushing and shoving me out of the way.

I often find myself falling into the same trap. Under stress and in a hurry to get to the next destination, I have missed way markers and got horribly lost.

A mind in a hurry and under stress will inevitably make mistakes. When under stress you go into tunnel vision, missing out on seeing many of the small miracles or the messages sent by the universe in your direction.

I have seen hikers stare ahead like a machine, hitting their walking sticks into the ground with a staccato aggressiveness, and not even responding to the friendly *buen camino* greeting from people along the way, very much in the same mode as if they were racing through a street in central London.

Sometimes a small talk with a villager or a word from a fellow pilgrim along the way can be an immense eye opener and blessing. I have walked several of the Camino routes more than twice and have been amazed at how much I didn't see the first time around, and how different each Camino walk was.

Staying in the moment is one of the most difficult exercises in the hurried life of the Western mind, which is preoccupied with all the fears of tomorrow and the events of the past.

Will I have to sleep under the bridge? Will I be safe? The negative self-talk can go on and on. I have seen pilgrims literally fall into panic upon hearing that there was no accommodation left in the town.

It is an innate fear to be in a foreign place and have no place to stay. Others stay completely calm, trusting in the universe that a solution will always be found, and laughing it off as part of the Camino experience.

A day can be ruined by a stressed-out, hurried mindset where one little catastrophe follows the next. You had a bad night and got up too late. In the hurry to get to the train station you forgot the ticket at home. You go back and take the next train. You miss an important appointment.

The mindset by this time is tuned to the mantra that "this is a really a bad day" and guess what? You are programming your mind and your day will not be good.

Going too fast is not allowing for a relaxed breathing rhythm that is crucial for a calm mind.

Many of us stressed-out folk believe that a good run or a hard work-out at the gym after a hard day at work will relieve the stress.

The opposite will be true if you exhaust your body during the exercise and don't go at such a pace that your breathing is still calm enough that you could have a normal conversation without gasping for breath.

By discovering your own pace and inner rhythm you will start breaking through that veil of hypnotism caused by years of exterior influences that is not really you.

Breaking through that veil and going into alignment strengthens self-confidence and that has an immediate effect on how you are perceived by others.

We become aware of who we are by becoming aware of our intrinsic emotions and feelings without making anyone else responsible.

This self-acceptance leads to self-love and an assertive life of self-determination, as opposed to a life determined by external factors that are seemingly out of our control.

Lack of self-esteem and self-doubt are very often caused by external triggers to which we have become programmed through self-hypnotic negative inner voices that often have their roots in over-critical parents, associates, so-called friends, marriage partners, colleagues or superiors.

Raised consciousness and alignment allow us to transform this negativity into a positive mindset that starts with self-acceptance and self-love, which will always manifest itself to the world around you.

You start taking control of your life as you start perceiving who you really are as opposed to an image you are trying to follow.

Hoping for happiness to come into your life is an illusion. If you are not grateful for the things in your life now you will not be grateful for the things waiting to come into your life.

Happiness is essentially how you manage your life in dealing with the natural cycle of ups and downs and how best you can pull yourself out of a down cycle back into a positive outlook.

Positive self-affirmation empowers you to be the real you. We are far too critical with ourselves.

In wanting to walk more in a day and comparing ourselves with others who are seemingly more fit, more beautiful and have more stamina, we lose our inner rhythm and pace.

Some of the questions that will arise:

Who am I really? Who am I at this moment in time? How can I best look after myself and my body? What are my real needs?

The Essentials:
- Walk slowly and with mindfulness.
- You are more likely to lose your way and make mistakes when you are in a hurry.
- Watch your breathing. Is it relaxed and coming from the lower belly?

- Find your own pace and rhythm. Don't be drawn by what the crowd does.

Chapter 15

Whispers from the Universe

W alking has influenced some of the world's most creative and talented artists throughout the centuries.

On the Camino Primitivo, or primitive route, from the Asturian capital of Oviedo to the ancient Roman town of Lugo, I happened to find a beautiful medieval chapel with Bach music playing from a concealed sound system.

A fellow pilgrim from the United States was deeply moved, telling me, "I can feel God in that music."

From what we know today, many of Bach's greatest works were probably inspired during long walks in nature.

He often went on long walks on foot through Germany. It is said that Bach's first major journey probably took place in early 1700, just before his fifteenth birthday. He walked some 375 kilometers (233 miles) from Ohrdruf to the northern town of Lueneburg (a distance of nearly 200 miles) to take up schooling.

His longest walk was the 378 kilometer (260 mile) journey from Arnstadt, in the state of Thuringia, to the Baltic port city of Luebeck in 1705 to hear the famous organist Dietrich Buxtehude.

Bach very much followed a "wander" (hiking) tradition that is still very much alive in Germany to this day. A journey on foot was not only a physical exercise but a way of self-development, improvement and personal growth.

The "wanderschaft" tradition traces its roots to the Middle Ages where part of the apprenticeship of a handyman is the journey on foot in search of aspects of the craft not known locally.

British sculptor and land artist Richard Long uses his walks in nature as art and is quoted as saying: "If you undertake a walk, you are echoing the whole history of mankind."

Merlin Coverley, author of *The Art of Wandering*, claims that walking and writing are one activity, with many famous writers like William Blake and Jean-Jacques Rousseau exploring their inner worlds with walking revealing the secrets of the subconscious.

Ernest Hemingway used walking as a way of working out issues in his writing. "I would walk along the quais when I had finished work or when I was trying to think something out," he wrote in *A Moveable Feast*.

Henry David Thoreau wrote in his journal, "Methinks that the moment my legs begin to move, my thoughts begin to flow.

The poet William Wordsworth was said to have walked as many as a 290,000 kilometers (180,000 miles) in his lifetime. This translates to an average of six and a half miles a day starting from the age of five.

Walking in our own rhythm and pace seems to create a natural feedback loop between the body and mental state, which you don't experience when behind the wheel of a car or on a bicycle.

It seems that the pace of the feet naturally vacillates with mood and the cadence of inner speech or subconscious mind.

A Stanford University study found that across the board, creativity levels were consistently higher for those people walking compared to those sitting.

"Many people anecdotally claim they do their best thinking when walking. We finally may be taking a step, or two, toward discovering why," Oppezzo and Schwartz wrote in the study published in the *Journal of Experimental Psychology: Learning, Memory and Cognition.*

"We already know that physical activity is important and sitting too often is unhealthy. This study is another justification for integrating bouts of physical activity into the day, whether it's recess at school or turning a meeting at work into a walking one," Oppezzo said. "We'd be healthier, and maybe more innovative for it."

A growing number of studies are also finding that spending time in green spaces—like parks, forest or gardens—can rejuvenate the mental resources that man-made environments deplete.

It's obvious that a city environment with traffic noise, blaring music and sirens is taking much more energy from you than an environment where you can hear birds singing, the rustling of leaves in the trees and the distant rush of water from a spring.

When our senses are attuned we can connect with the universe, God or the higher energy.

It is that moment on the Camino, after you have walked things off after a couple of days, that you begin to feel alive.

Your walk has become sprightly, easy and effortless. You fall into an inner mode of relaxed consciousness where the mind is no longer occupied with negative self-talk.

I've been amazed how even the world of nature starts reacting to this higher energy frequency. Robins are normally shy birds but I was utterly amazed one morning when such a bird perched itself on the breakfast table, only a few centimeters away, breaking into a beautiful song.

I have been followed by stray dogs and cats seeking attention. Donkeys and horses come closer to greet you as you go walking past.

Nothing like this has happened to me when I was engaged in negative and self-absorbing thoughts.

During such "empty spaces" I have made some of my deepest spiritual experiences on the Camino, where I have meanwhile become absolutely convinced that there is a higher intelligence, working as a creator both within and without.

Our world is exceedingly complex and chaotic but behind everything we know there is a natural order of things that cannot just be a coincidence.

In contrast to religious doctrine, spirituality is experiential and a deeply personal connection with the divine. In simple terms: God cannot be believed. God can only be experienced.

Religion is a belief system and a code of conduct developed by man. It is denominational and there are rules you have to follow.

Religious ritual can be a method for attainment of the spiritual. There is enormous energy that can be generated by groups of people praying and singing together.

At its best religion is a ritualized expression of the spiritual. At its worst it becomes an instrument of dehumanization and control.

As the author and priest Richard Rohr wrote in an essay:

"If people do not go beyond first level metaphors, rituals, and comprehension, most religions seem to end up with a God who is often angry, petulant, needy, jealous, and who will love us only if we are 'worthy' and belonging to the correct group…

"God and the history of religion seem to prefer mandates, coercion, blame, and shame to achieve some kind of supposed transformation. This is quite helpful for social order and control of the immature, I really understand that. But it is quite clear to me, in the later years of my life, that God does not love me *if* I change, but God loves me so *that* I can change. That is an entirely different agenda."

Rohr goes on to say that it is almost the job description of religion for "excluding, expelling, and excommunicating."

He quotes Simone Weil, who said, "The problem with Christianity is that it insists on seeing itself as a separate religion, instead of as a healing message for all religions."

"I am afraid that is what will always emerge when you have religion without spirituality, or pious practices without inner experience. The very best thing will then become the very worst thing, and the only way *through* is to 'be awakened and astonished' by a divine love that is of an utterly new dimension," Rohr writes in his essay.

It is something I have personally grappled with all my life. Growing up in apartheid South Africa, I could never comprehend how white people, even family members, would profess to be devout Christians, while treating fellow human beings—people of different color with the utmost contempt and hate—sometimes only hours after attending communion.

I hear until today the screams of the black laborer whipped mercilessly by an uncle in a farm shed. I was still a child but the screams cut into my body like I myself was being beaten. It was an epiphany. I knew instinctively that this was wrong. No man had the right to beat another like that. The seeds were sown for a growing political activism against an evil system. If people could be all pious and religious one day and act so differently the next, something was wrong with this religion.

The roots of apartheid indeed go back to a perverted religious belief of a racial hierarchy and that the white Afrikaner nation was a people chosen by God to subordinate other ethnic groups.

It is a false interpretation of an Old Testament extract in the Book of Genesis where Ham, the son of Noah, is cursed by his father for a serious transgression—in that all his descendants shall be slaves and water bearers. Ham is often cited by racists as the father of the black race although there is no biblical or other evidence of this. As happens so often, extracts of the scriptures are twisted to justify an ideology.

Something is wrong with organized religion when its leaders turn a blind eye for decades to the abhorrent cases of child sexual abuse by priests, nuns and members of religious orders.

Studies have found that the hierarchical structures and mandatory celibacy in the Catholic Church was a major precipitating risk factor for child abuse, and that popes and bishops created a culture of secrecy, leading to gross failures in transparency, accountability and openness.

As Rohr put it, "Religion brings out the best and the worst in mankind."

The positive side of organized religion is that a powerful energy can emanate from a large group of people in a congregation or gathering that unite in prayer or meditation.

But do we need in our age people to tell us *You have to believe what I believe?*

We need to go back to the mystical roots of Christianity, which is built around the figure of Jesus, who fought the hypocrisy of religion as practiced by the scribes and the Pharisees of the time.

He was the ultimate spiritual teacher, who realized that human suffering cannot be alleviated by abiding by certain codes of religious conduct but only from a transformation of inner attitude, action and thought.

Fundamentalist preachers for centuries have read the scriptures literally, taking many extracts out of context to exert influence and power. The images and mythology behind many biblical stories open up an entirely different world and multi-layered interpretations.

Conventional Christian doctrine has it that Jesus was conceived and born of his mother Mary while she was still a virgin, and she remained a virgin all her life. However, the story of the Virgin Birth is deeply embedded in mythology, going back about 2,000 years before the birth of Jesus. Mut-em-ua, the virgin Queen of Egypt, was said to have given birth to the Pharaoh Amenkept (or Amenophis) III, who built the temple of Luxor.

The Egyptian God Ra (or Sun) was said to have been born of a virgin mother called Nut.

Religious belief throughout the ages has originated from the depths of the human psyche and collective unconscious.

The concept of the birth of the divine child is found in Krishna, Buddha, Mithra, Horus and Dionysus.

Spiritual transformation of body and mind is at the heart of many religions. Concepts such as the divine birth, being born again and the resurrection, then, are filled with many different layers of meanings.

The entire creation process is evolutionary and about change. God or the universe wants us to develop, transform and grow to a higher consciousness.

While religion focuses on who you are supposed to be by abiding by certain rules of conduct and practice, spirituality is all about becoming who you really are with all your unique, individual, God-given potentials and abilities.

The renowned vocal artist, educationalist and motivational speaker Pastor Wintley Phipps describes religion as the focus on the big three: believing, behaving and belonging, while forgetting the fourth pillar— becoming, the becoming of who you are truly meant to be in terms of God's destiny.

It is why so many hundreds of thousands of people are walking the Camino. Most of the people I have spoken to on my walks would describe themselves as spiritual seekers rather than followers of a certain religious doctrine.

In becoming mindful and watchful for the subtle messages of the universe transmitted in dreams, images and symbols, life takes on an entirely different meaning.

We are on the brink of another raised level of human consciousness which is non-divisive, universalist, tolerant, self-reflective and compassionate.

At the same time elementary and revolutionary changes are always confronted with a backlash from those defending the old order.

In recent years we have seen a frightening rise of movements seeking to divide and separate with fear-instilling messages, propounded by dangerous narcissistic and ego-driven leaders.

It is the natural pendulum of the yin and the yang. Energy is wasted in the hysteria over the actions coming from the shadow.

In going with the higher frequency of the raised consciousness, the danger is that we react with the same patterns as our adversaries. We also become hateful, ranting and vengeful.

Yet when seen according to the law of opposites that is the foundation of life, a different perspective can be taken. Identity is defined in terms of the opposite and it is often when confronted with the extreme opposite that we are galvanized into action.

The Essentials:

- Walking creates a natural feedback loop between the mental state and the body.
- Walking is inspiration and a creative process, connecting with the higher self and aligning with the universe.
- When our senses are attuned to nature we create a connection to the universe. There is a natural order between the seemingly chaotic.
- God cannot be believed. He can only be experienced.
- There are big differences between religion and spirituality. Religion is a doctrine. Spirituality is individual experience.

Chapter 16

Gratitude

There is a saying that if you aren't grateful for the things you have now, you will never be grateful for the things you are wishing for. Being grateful for what you already have is a key aspect of happiness.

It is not about mumbling off five daily gratitudes like a "must-do happiness ritual" but really exploring that which you are truly grateful for.

"I'm so grateful that I have been given the opportunity by the universe to do this walk, that I'm healthy enough to do it and that I have been given the time and the financial means."

You feel that gratitude energy flow like a wave through every cell of your body in one big exhaling breath, while you move your lips into a gentle smile.

The advanced spiritual teachers even give thanks for the unfortunate events that come into their lives, because they view this as an opportunity for the soul to grow.

Most prayer emphasizes the wanting of something: better health, finding a job, a marriage partner, getting out of debt, having more money, or a new home. This often comes out of a feeling of privation and deficiency.

Expressing gratitude in a prayer comes with an entirely different mindset of abundance, empowerment, and the wisdom that all is grace and interwoven within the bigger matrix of higher meaning.

Gratitude comes from within and it is entirely different from the consumer-oriented mindset, which is insatiable and never satisfied.

Being grateful puts things into perspective and gives true meaning to being grateful for every day where we are healthy, breathing and alive.

I met several people on the Camino who gave me a new sense of meaning when they told me of their own battles.

On my first Camino, I met a cheerful, lanky guy from Scotland in his early 60s. Only later did I find out that he had locked the door of his home, and on the spur of the moment walked all the way through England, France and Spain. It was his way of dealing with the grief of losing his beloved wife to cancer.

A man who had most of his intestines removed in a cancer surgery and had walked with me for several days taught me the preciousness and gratitude of living every moment to the fullest.

A young man was told by doctors two years prior to his walk that he would probably never walk again after his spine was fractured in several places in a mountain bike accident. And here he was on the Camino, walking strong, up to 40 kilometers (24.8 miles) a day.

Another pilgrim, who had been diagnosed with multiple sclerosis—a potentially disabling disease of the central nervous system—was walking the Camino, grateful for every step he could take without pain.

Hearing these stories from fellow pilgrims made my own problems seem like minor difficulties, especially now in writing these words and looking back in time.

Verbally expressing our gratitude or even writing it down in a gratitude diary increases our energy, optimism and feeling of general well-being.

Researchers at the Nottingham University in England found that the kind of gratitude people practice or feel influences how much they give back.

Individuals with a broader outlook of gratitude –who are more likely to notice and appreciate the positive in the world—are more likely to engage in behaviors that help others, compared with those who feel gratitude as a temporary emotion that passes.

These people also experience greater resilience in stress situations.

Feeling grateful helps people to reciprocate that feeling.

Gratitude had the largest effect on people's willingness to give back—more than sadness, happiness, empathy, shame and anger, according to the research.

However, recent research has determined that gratitude toward our close relationship partners serves the additional purpose of helping to strengthen those bonds.

Gratitude helps us notice and attend to the positive, responsive behaviors that our loved ones enact toward us. It could be a time when your partner made dinner or a friend did you a favor.

It is especially beneficial in our relationships when those important people in our lives are responsive to our needs and deserving of our gratitude.

The Zulu term ubuntu aptly describes that we are who we are because of those who have formed us during the course of our lives.

Ubuntu stems from the Zulu phrase: "Umuntu ngumuntu ngabantu," which literally means that a person is a person through other people.

It very much affirms what is becoming the era of raised human consciousness.

Whatever we are and whatever we have comes from the greater whole and from that stems individual responsibility for the greater whole.

Some of the world's wealthiest and greatest philanthropists have understood this concept very well.

It's the law of reciprocity which we find in the Bible verse Luke 6:38: "If you give to others, you will be given a full amount in return. It will be packed down, shaken together, and spilling over into your lap. The way you treat others is the way you will be treated."

It means much more than giving in order to receive back, and goes far beyond individual or egotistical reasons. A greater humanity results in a reciprocal culture of giving and receiving, of which the material things are only one small part.

We all need to be kind to each other. It costs nothing to be polite and kind. It is a human quality that unfortunately is getting increasingly lost in the hurried pace of our modern lives.

All too often I have seen people on the Camino ignore the people who greeted them with a friendly "buen camino." It is human decency and kindness to respond.

A friendly smile with the simple greeting of "Hola" and thank you, "Gracias," in the local language immediately creates a positive resonance.

Nothing in this world is permanent, and very often we only realize in retrospect when we have lost the people or the things that we took for granted how important they were in our lives.

We humans are programmed to live either in the future or in the past, missing the magic and the appreciation of the moment.

The Camino has taught me in so many ways to be grateful to others for seemingly small things: the farmer waiting at the hill to fill water bottles of exhausted pilgrims in the midday heat, the stranger who took us to the next town in his car when all accommodation in the town was occupied, and the kind old granny who took me by the hand to walk with me a kilometer to the next way marker after I had gotten lost.

The Essentials:

- Be grateful for everything, especially the small things.
- Express your gratitude verbally, write it down or keep a gratitude diary.
- A feeling of gratitude comes from within and needs to be felt.
- We are who we are because of what we have received from others and the greater whole.
- Give back.

Chapter 17

Choosing Your Friends

J im Rohn, the American entrepreneur, motivational speaker and author, once said, "You are the average of the five people you spend the most time with."

Humans are social beings and over time we will subconsciously adopt the mannerisms of speech, posture, thoughts and even dress code of the people we spend most of our time with.

It is therefore of crucial importance to make a checklist of those people who positively encourage you, who have your real interest at heart or who pull you down.

Numerous people on the Camino, especially women, told me of the huge obstacles they had to overcome with husbands, parents, siblings, friends and even children who tried to dissuade them from walking the Camino.

Very often those people closest to you pull you down when they hear you talk of an "outlandish" business idea, or going on that trip you have dreamed about taking for so long.

When you move to a higher energy frequency and start becoming strong, those people around you, who are still stuck in their comfort zone, will feel challenged and threatened. They want you to stay at the same level they are at. Change is frightening, especially if you see it happening to people you love.

If you take time out to walk the Camino in Spain for a four- or five-week period, you will come back a changed person.

Many pilgrims find it very difficult to fall back into the same old rhythm they left prior to walking the Camino. Much the same happened to me after my first long walk, lasting almost five weeks.

I realized that I had to radically change the life I had been living up to then. That included breaking out of an unhappy marriage, leaving an unfulfilling and highly stressful job, and doing an inventory of the people and things influencing me negatively.

We have many associates but when it comes down to it, we have very few real friends who truly understand us and are supportive of our soul growth process.

Fellow pilgrims, who shared the deep spiritual experiences after returning from the Camino, were sometimes ridiculed by friends or family members. My advice, therefore: Be careful who you open up to. Few people are genuinely interested. Most people are just curious or have hidden motives.

Sometimes it is better to keep that most precious experience secret in your heart.

We often stay too long in relationships that have long outlived their purpose. The question that needs to be asked is: Do I feel comfortable, uplifted and energized when I'm in the company of that person? Or do I feel emotionally drained, exhausted and in a bad mood after spending time with him or her?

Who is your main reference group that influences you on many levels? Every so often it might be necessary to reflect on this.

It's not that you want to hurt and exclude some people from your life. But the time might have come just to spend much less time with them and to spend more time with those people who really uplift you.

A good exercise is: Who are the five people you would choose to live with on a lonely island? Who are the people you would only want to spend a weekend with? Who are the three-minute people you want to remain polite with but keep at a clear distance?

A good guideline is the content of your conversations. Are you sharing uplifting ideas and thoughts or are you spending your time gossiping about other people and wallowing in negative things that happened in the past?

People's happiness depends on the happiness of others with whom they are connected, according to a Harvard University study on happiness by James H. Fowler and Nicholas A. Christakis.

They determined clusters of happy and unhappy people in the networks they surrounded themselves with, and were particularly interested in whether the spread of happiness pertains not just to direct relationships (such as friends) but also to indirect relationships (such as friends of friends) and whether there are geographical or temporal constraints on the spread of happiness through a social network.

While most research on the topic has focused on genetic and geographical reasons for people's happiness, this study added that happiness is a network phenomenon, clustering in groups of people that extend up to three degrees of separation (for example, to one's friends' friends' friends).

Because we humans are so interdependent and dependent on each other, we want to be validated and get those accolades from our neighbors and friends.

It is easier to follow the crowd than to go against it. We pick up the good and the bad habits from the people we surround ourselves with.

Low-achieving students who befriended high achievers had greater academic success than those who spent time with other low-achieving students. Surround yourself with successful and happy people and the likelihood of that rubbing off on you is pretty big.

The opposite is just as true. Alcohol and substance abuse is closely connected to your social crowd.

I have met some of the nicest, most intelligent, wise and successful people on the Camino. It is not the ordinary type of man or woman who decides to make such an epic journey of self-discovery.

I did also meet the odd person who was totally inconsiderate, impolite and generally acting out like a total jerk. I had to ask myself what they were looking for on the Camino, where it's all about sharing and being kind and respectful of each other's space.

The crowds get bigger as you get closer toward Santiago. It's almost a rule of thumb that the bigger the crowd the less mindful the individual. Way markers are defaced with graffiti, empty bottles and other rubbish are left by the wayside, and groups of cyclists have no shame in forcing pilgrims with heavy backpacks off the path, telling them in no uncertain terms to make room with incessant ringing of bicycle bells.

These, in my mind, are not pilgrims but day tourists who go home to brag to their friends that they have been on the Camino.

A large number of people unfortunately live behind the veil of fulfilling primarily the most basic of human needs, showing total disregard for the environment and fellow living beings.

It poses the question: How do I deal with the negativity that comes my way and over which I have no control?

Very often when we experience something negative we stay with it far too long. A lovely Zen story goes like this:

Two traveling monks reached a town where there was a young woman waiting to step out of her sedan chair. The rains had made deep puddles and she couldn't step across without spoiling her silken robes. She stood there, looking very cross and impatient. She was scolding her attendants. They had nowhere to place the packages they held for her, so they couldn't help her across the puddle.

The younger monk noticed the woman, said nothing, and walked by. The older monk quickly picked her up and put her on his back, transported her across the water, and put her down on the other side. She didn't thank the older monk; she just shoved him out of the way and departed.

As they continued on their way, the young monk was brooding and pre-occupied. After several hours, unable to hold his silence, he spoke out. "That woman back there was very selfish and rude, but you picked her up on your back and carried her! Then she didn't even thank you!

"I set the woman down hours ago," the older monk replied. "Why are you still carrying her?"

As we become more aware of soul purpose and soul destiny we need to become more aware of what depletes our energy. We need to let go and realize that we are unable to change those people who have wronged us or are misbehaving. We have only control our thoughts about these people.

Spending time on anger, resentment and the sadness over the other person being non-receptive means that we have less energy for that which is really important in living out our full potential.

The Essentials:

- Choose your friends wisely.
- Make a checklist of "associates" and real friends.
- You adopt the good and bad habits, beliefs, and mannerisms of the people you spend the most time with.
- Happiness is contagious, especially if you surround yourself with upbeat and positive people.
- Let go of negativity thrown at you by people whose behavior you cannot change or control.

Chapter 18
Being Kind

It's always a happy moment on the Camino when a total stranger greets you with a friendly: "Buen Camino," wishing you a pleasant journey.

It never ceases to amaze how friendly and courteous the Spanish people are toward the thousands of pilgrims walking the Camino each year.

An African priest with a smiling demeanor comes over toward us, greeting every single guest in the café with a handshake and wishing them a good day with a beaming smile.

The energy in the café immediately changes to a higher energy frequency, with happy, smiling people all around. A small act like a heartfelt greeting can remain etched in memory for a lifetime.

Being kind, friendly and courteous costs nothing but makes a big difference in how we feel in the public space.

It's a way of practicing to be nice. A smile opens doors and may I see many doors to signing a business deal or a good job.

Typical character traits of a kind person are:

- Giving rather than taking.
- Showing appreciation even for small things like holding open a door.
- Trustworthiness. Their word counts. They value friendships and relationships.
- Seeing the positive rather than the negative.
- They don't interrupt you in mid-sentence and are really capable of deep-listening.
- Warm-heartedness. You just like being around them.
- Empathy and compassion.
- They don't boast about their achievements.
- They see the bigger picture rather than their own personal ego needs.
- Unconditional helpfulness, without expecting anything in return.

It is much more difficult to be kind than rude, demanding maturity where often a spontaneous emotional reaction is triggered or your positive mood is shifted following insignificant actions by others.

When you are out of alignment you will find offense in pretty much everything people around you are doing or the environment in which you are currently moving.

It is the mature character who understands a situation, rather than reacting with the same energy or trying to retaliate against the person who was responsible for the hurt.

However, a common misconception is that being kind is allowing people to ride roughshod over your own boundaries.

A healthy self-awareness is drawing a clear boundary for people, situations, events and outside influences that draw you down into the lower energy frequency of negativity.

Very often people unable to draw a clear boundary for others are also unaware when they are crossing the boundary of others—especially true of the narcissistic character.

A kind person is the opposite of the narcissistic and self-centered character, who has an exaggerated sense of self-importance and entitlement.

The narcissistic character unfortunately has especially come to the fore in our age of social media with the addiction to "likes" on Facebook. They will always post pictures showing themselves in the best light and are addicted to accolades.

The narcissist has a highly inflated sense of self-importance. He is constantly telling you how many kilometers he walked that day and how fast he reached the next town to grab that first bed in the hostel. He is better than everyone else and has no qualms in making everyone aware of it.

They are sometimes not that easy to detect because they come across at first as being very charming and dashing personalities. But they will inevitably turn every conversation to themselves. Even when they open up to bad events that happened in their lives, they will inevitably always blame others for that misfortune. They cannot and will not take responsibility for their own actions and behaviors.

Beware if they tell you of their life history of wrecked and destructive relationships for which, of course, it was always the others who were responsible.

Dr. Jean Twenge and W. Keith Campbell, in their book *The Narcissism Epidemic*, describe how the alarming rise of narcissism and vanity is having a catastrophic effect at every level of society.

In an age of entitlement, narcissism is causing a massive fallout, spinning people into loneliness, debt and depression, according to the two authors.

We are seeing in the major industrial countries a breakdown in civility or civilized conduct in the public arena.

Social norms and rituals are the glue that holds our social fabric together, especially those that feel under threat by uncontrollable external influences.

In the age of the narcissism epidemic, described by Twenge and Campbell, it never ceases to astound that basic manners and politeness in the public arena are getting lost. Teachers complain of the growing disrespect that children show toward them in the classroom. Passengers on trains, buses or airplanes are forced to listen to loud, blaring music. Elderly or disabled people are pushed aside in the rush to get a seat. Laws have to be passed to prohibit smoking in the public space because there is lack of mindfulness.

I have portrayed here the light and shadow aspects of two extreme personalities. In reality we all have aspects of both character traits.

Mixing with many different types of people from many different nationalities and backgrounds while walking the walk on the Camino is a good feedback mechanism.

In the hostels you sometimes have to share the most basic of amenities. You sleep in bunk beds in large rooms. Bathrooms and kitchens have to be shared with dozens of others. Pilgrims cook meals together, share first aid utensils, and help carry the backpack of a fellow pilgrim in pain.

Why go through the hassle, then, of sleeping in a pilgrims' hostel when you can find private accommodation in almost every town that is far more comfortable?

I have been in pilgrims' hostels with very wealthy business people, doctors, lawyers, and actors. All have said that staying in a pilgrims' hostel has taught them humility.

No lonely luxury hotel room can offer the camaraderie with fellow pilgrims in a hostel over a self-cooked meal, and the intense conversations over shared experiences.

You will soon realize how you come across with other people and whether strangers are open to bonding with you or will avoid you like the plague. The typical narcissist becomes a very lonely person and will hopefully go into some introspection.

The kind person is the person who is in the long run a success in all spheres of life. People don't do business with people they don't like. You choose a partner and a friend where there is natural empathy and kindness. You walk with people whose company you enjoy.

The question each one of us needs to ask on a daily basis: "Am I predominantly a giver or am I a taker?"

The Essentials:

- Kind people are givers. Narcissists are takers.
- A smile makes a difference.
- Show appreciation and respect.
- Be mindful of your habits in the public space.
- How people treat you is often a reflection of your mindset and attitude.

Chapter 19

Ancestral Roots

There is a long tradition on the Camino that reminded me a lot of the Zulu culture in South Africa.

Cultures rooted in tradition and ritual place great value on their history and ancestral roots. Much of this has been lost in the modern materialist world—which then finds an unhealthy avenue in extreme nationalism.

The Zulu greeting "sawbona" means "I see you," to which the fellow being greeted responds with "yebo," or "yes, and I see you too."

In the rural Zululand of my childhood the conversation would then continue with strangers exchanging their names and asking each other the names of their parents and grandparents and from what village they came from so that the ancestral tree to the tribe or clan could be recognized.

The Zulus journeyed mostly on foot, and would pile stone cairns at key junctions as a mark of respect to the ancestors and asking them for a safe journey. In the Umfolozi Game Reserve in KwaZulu-Natal there is a massive stone cairn that dates back to the Stone Age.

I was surprised to find this tradition also on the Camino in Spain and learned that similar rituals also exist in other cultures such as the Inuit, American Indians and Celts, from which the practice probably originates in Spain.

Since the beginning of time, stones have evoked a powerful imagery in mankind. Whether in the Tramuntana Mountains of Majorca or the red cliffs of Sedona in Arizona, the faces carved in rock by nature's tools were revered as holy sites by the ancient peoples.

One of the most powerful images is the stone of Jacob, or the Stone of Destiny, in the Book of Genesis. It was used as a pillow by Jacob when he fell asleep and had his dream of the stairway to heaven.

Jacob then poured oil on the rock and called the place Bethel or "Place of God." Several legends surround the stone, which was allegedly brought to Ireland by the Prophet Jeremiah, and from there to Scotland. Between 1308 and 1996 it rested in the British royal throne. But according to recent research the stone was probably of Scottish origin and not the real stone of Jacob.

Both Jews and Muslims believe that the first of God's creation was the foundation stone—the massive rock embedded under the Temple Mount in Jerusalem. It was the place where Jacob anointed the rock and where the Great Temple of Jerusalem was later built by King Solomon.

The corner or foundation stone of a new building to this day has an important symbolic significance.

Friends and family often give the pilgrim a stone for the journey on the Camino, which is left on a way marker or cairn along the route.

In medieval times it was common for one member of a family to walk the Camino to atone for the sins of the entire clan. The family would in return collect funds to finance the pilgrimage.

The pilgrimage began after crossing the threshold of his front door, and after being granted permission to leave by his local religious authorities. Before leaving he had attended mass, where his staff and scrip were blessed by the priest.

It would be months, sometimes more than a year, before he returned—if he was lucky. Many pilgrims did not survive the journey, making the ultimate sacrifice.

Along the Camino, the pilgrim would add a rock to the cairns along the wayside, saying a prayer for a member of the family, going down the line of the family tree, starting with the parents, siblings, grandparents, great-grandparents, and all the other members of the clan.

Today the tradition continues and many of the cairns have rocks with prayer inscriptions for a deceased loved one, someone going through a serious illness or a special wish.

I have found the ritual to be a powerful spiritual experience and many pilgrims report the same, like a relative contacting them soon after a stone had been placed for them on the cairn.

Connecting to the bloodline ancestors is the one pillar.

The Buddhist teacher Thich Nhat Hanh writes of the importance of connecting to the spiritual ancestors:

"There are many ways to offer the Dharma for a child to be born in his or her spiritual life, but the most usual is to share the Dharma through words. I try to practice in a way that allows me to touch my blood ancestors and my spiritual ancestors every day. Whenever I feel sad or a little fragile, I invoke their presence for support, and they never fail to be there (Hanh, Thich Nhat. *Living Buddha, Living Christ* (p. 48). Ebury Publishing. Kindle Edition).

When the Buddha was about to pass away, many of his disciples were upset that he would no longer be with them. So he reassured them by saying, "My physical body will no longer be here, but my teaching body, Dharmakaya, will always be with you" (Hanh, Thich Nhat. *Living Buddha, Living Christ* (p. 50). Ebury Publishing. Kindle Edition).

In Christianity the difference is made between the historical and the living Jesus. The historical Jesus is the man who was born in Bethlehem over 2000 years ago and died on the cross when he was a young man in his early 30s. The living Jesus is touched within our hearts when we live and practice his teachings and prayers, true to his saying:

"Whenever two or three are gathered in my name, I will be there."

The living Christ within is living a life where there is active practicing of loving kindness, tolerance and compassion.

According to Hanh, "When we understand and practice deeply the life and teachings of Buddha or the life and teachings of Jesus, we penetrate the door and enter the abode of the living Buddha and the living Christ, and life eternal presents itself to us" (Hanh, Thich Nhat. *Living Buddha, Living Christ* (p. 56). Ebury Publishing. Kindle Edition).

Living on the fast track we forget who we are at heart because the gateways to our souls are wide open to a daily wave of negativity, fear-instilling, and violent images.

Many people in our modern world are so stressed out that they could be compared to pressure valves waiting to explode.

Much value is placed on cultural identity. But culture is constantly exposed to change and exterior influences. The Nazis propounded the concept of an Aryan, or master, race to set themselves apart from other nations and ethnic groups. But thanks to genetics we know that the concept in itself is totally flawed. Humanity is a mixture of all races and nationalities.

Genetic research is still a young science but some scientists believe that some of our habits, traumas, memories and survival instincts are imprinted in our genes from our ancestors.

An ancestor born centuries ago could still be impacting your life. Ancestral memories could be passed on for 14 generations, according to one body of research.

A study by the European Molecular Biology Organization looked at *C. elegans* nematodes, types of roundworms with very short lifespans. The researchers genetically engineered them to carry a glowing gene, a protein that fluoresced, so they could track it under UV light.

They then placed the worms in a cold environment and watched as the gene glowed, but dimly. Moving them to a warm environment, they saw the gene glow far more brightly. When they were moved back to the cold room, the gene continued to glow, which suggested the "memory" of the warm environment was maintained.

When these worms reproduced, this memory, via this glowing gene, was passed on through an unprecedented 14 generations, no matter whether they received it via eggs or sperm. The offspring would be "aware" of the warm environment even without having experienced it themselves.

Grandchildren of Holocaust survivors have been found reliving the trauma of their grandparents and to have lower stress-resilience levels.

A great grandchild develops the same music or art skills as an ancestor long dead without much training. Similar career paths sometimes go through generations.

We are who we are not only because of the influences of our immediate friends and the environment in which we live, but it also appears that some of our habits, fears and talents are inherited from our ancestors.

This poses the question: Are our long-dead ancestors influencing our lives in more ways than one?

Do our dead ancestors or loved ones intervene, sometimes in vivid dreams, especially in those times when we are in desperate need of help?

The English singer-songwriter and former Beatle Paul McCartney has an especially poignant story of how the lyrics of his famous song "Let it Be" originated:

"I was exhausted! Some nights I'd go to bed and my head would just flop on the pillow; and when I'd wake up I'd have difficulty pulling it off, thinking, 'Good job I woke up just then or I might have suffocated.'

"Then one night, somewhere between deep sleep and insomnia, I had the most comforting dream about my mother, who died when I was only 14. She had been a nurse, my mum, and very hardworking, because she wanted the best for us. We weren't a well-off family—we didn't have a car, we just about had a television—so both of my parents went out to work, and Mum contributed a good half to the family income. At night when she came home, she would cook, so we didn't have a lot of time with each other. But she was just a very comforting presence in my life. And when she died, one of the difficulties I had, as the years went by, was that I couldn't recall her face so easily. That's how it is for everyone, I think. As each day goes by, you just can't bring their face into your mind; you have to use photographs and reminders like that.

"So in this dream twelve years later, my mother appeared, and there was her face, completely clear, particularly her eyes, and she said to me very gently, very reassuringly: 'Let it be...

"So, being a musician, I went right over to the piano and started writing a song: 'When I find myself in times of trouble, Mother Mary comes to me'...Mary was my mother's name...

"'Speaking words of wisdom, let it be. There will be an answer, let it be.' It didn't take long. I wrote the main body of it in one go, and then the subsequent verses developed from there:

"When all the broken-hearted people living in the world agree, there will be an answer, let it be."

I have no scientific or rational explanation, but I believe that in some ways we are connected to those loved ones that have passed on. It appears there is a window from the other side where the deceased sometimes reach out to us.

I've had several almost lucid dreams where my beloved grandparents have reached out to me in very much the same way that Paul McCartney describes in his dream. The theme has always been in a similar vein: "Remain in faith and trust. Everything is going to be fine."

In one dream during a particularly stressful period in my life, I was again the little boy aged three or four years, where I felt the warm hand of my grandmother, almost with uncanny reality, comforting a frightened child.

While working on this book my younger brother died unexpectedly from a heart attack. He did not have an easy life, haunted for many years by the trauma of the time he spent as a soldier in the South African army during the war in Angola. In the lucid, vividly clear dream, I saw family members and friends at the funeral writing words of appreciation for my brother on stones they placed on a table in a darkened room. Then I saw my brother in the background walking about, seemingly confused. Surprised that he was still among us, I went up to him, telling him, "You aren't supposed to be here." Sunlight penetrated through a skylight window, and I continued, "Just follow the light. Follow the light. You will be ok."

I believe that our soul is eternal. When we are born we are like a droplet taken from the ocean and return to that ocean when we die. On a microscopic level we are all molecules coming from the stars.

Much of the craziness around us can be attributed to the alienation from both the spiritual and the cultural roots of the bloodline. Every culture needs to rediscover the rituals and traditions that served so many of the generations that went before.

The Essentials:

- Is there a common theme or issue in your family going back generations?
- Being aware of our ancestors gives us a sense of purpose and belonging.
- Be grateful for all those who lived before you.
- You carry within you the seeds of the past and the future.
- Be proud of your cultural heritage and identity.

Chapter 20

Respect for the Sacred

H umanity will only survive when we recognize that the sacred within is also the sacred without.

Respect for that which is holy and sacred is closely aligned to respect for the self and self-love.

It is telling for humanity that the sacred house in which we live is being treated with such lack of mindfulness.

When you walk for hours along a country road you realize how many tons of rubbish including plastic bags, tin cans, plastic bottles and cigarette butts are carelessly thrown out of car windows by passing motorists.

It has a devastating effect on other living beings. I've seen cows munch plastic bags and hedgehogs trapped in trash left at the roadside.

Much can be attributed to the disconnect of modern man from his natural surroundings. Nature is a manifestation of God and not without reason have the wise teachers of old described time spent in nature as our best healer.

Any person who has spent alone time in the African bush or hiked alone for hours in pristine nature will soon become aware of the awesome marvel of creation and the interconnectedness of all living beings. God can be seen at work in slow motion.

But never before in the history of mankind have we seen such a rate of extinction of biological and animal species. The ocean waters are being polluted with plastics and the atmosphere brought into imbalance with excess burning of fossil fuels.

For centuries Christianity has had a false understanding of man's role in nature based on misinterpretation of the Old Testament of the Bible in Genesis 1:28, in which man is given the cultural mandate to subdue and rule over the earth:

"And God blessed them, and God said unto them, be fruitful, and multiply, and replenish the earth, and subdue it: and have dominion over the fish of the sea, and over the fowl of the air, and over every living thing that (Heb. *creepeth*) moveth upon the earth."

Especially the translations of "subdue" and "dominion" from the Hebrew have different meanings. Rather than exploitation and domination, the call to humanity by God is like that to a king to take care of the weak and poor in his kingdom. Man is called to preserve the natural beauty of the environment entrusted to him and to restore those places that have been harshly affected by force and hardness of rule.

The lost gospel of St. Thomas, discovered in Egypt in the 1940s, has a far more mystical approach to many of the biblical interpretations. Rather waiting for the Second Coming of the Christ, the lesson espoused here is all about nurturing and discovering the Christ Within—closely resembling what is described in Buddhism as discovering the Buddha Nature.

The Medieval interpretation of Nature was that of a harsh alien environment that needed to be conquered. Paradise and a life of bliss could only be expected after death and resurrection.

In contrast the eastern Taoist tradition is all about yielding to the laws of nature. The philosophy of the Five Elements in essence is about the right timing in accordance with the laws of nature. The harmony of objects and things in Feng Shui, the cultivation of the life-force energy of Chi in the body with nutrition, Qi Gong and Tai Chi and the ancient Book of Wisdom, the I Qing, all are built on the foundations of the Elements.

Wood, associated with spring, is the period for planting; Fire is the heat of summer when the plants begin to expand and grow; Earth or late summer is the period for harvesting; Metal, autumn, is the beginning of withdrawal and Water is the time for withdrawal and reflection. Each element can also be associated with episodes of a lifetime or birth signs. The ancient Chinese rulers were very circumspect in consulting the I Qing before they took major decisions like negotiating or going to war with an opponent.

Likewise, the Greek, Roman and Medieval cultures placed great emphasis on building their temples and cities in harmony with the natural environment. These cultures were still steeped in myth and legend, while the modern world is dominated by the economic.

Modern man's environment—often in an urban concrete jungle–is very much a contributing factor to the alienation from nature. When man builds without connection to nature, everything is rectangular and purpose-oriented.

We know from much research that the suburbs in which people live determine their lifespan, the level and quality of their education and health, and the possibility of committing a crime or falling victim to violence.

Ancient man was still very much connected to the worship of the sacred in the natural environment. Millions of people visit the special sacred places on earth, telling stories of extraordinary experience and even healing from serious illness after sensing the miraculous.

Among the most famous are the Temple Mount in Jerusalem, the Giza plateau in Egypt, Lourdes in France, Mecca in Saudi Arabia and the Kashi Vishwanath Temple in India.

Several faiths including the Buddhist, Hindu, Jain and Bon have a special connection to Mount Kailash in Tibet. Thousands of people go on a pilgrimage around the mountain every year as a way to spiritual purification.

The Shamanic Bon religion believes the mountain is the abode of the sky goddess Sipaimen and it is considered the central pillar of the world.

Uluru, or Ayers Rock, in Australia is sacred to the Aboriginal people, who believe that the mountain was created at the beginning of time by ten ancestors or spirit people of the Aboriginals.

Victoria Falls in Zimbabwe is one of the seven natural wonders of the world. The local people called it Mosi-oa-Tunya or the "smoke that thunders." The baTonga and Nambya tribes in the area believe the Zambezi River and the waterfalls have a connection to their ancestral spirits.

The river spirit called Nyaminyami controls the Zambezi, and anyone interfering with the natural flow of the water would be punished.

Most of Europe's ancient cathedrals and chapels were built on places sacred to mankind since earliest times.

The oldest chapel on the Spanish island of Majorca, San Miguel, dates back to the 13th century but was built on a site used by pagans and Muslims for religious worship for many centuries prior to that. It lies close to one of Europe's most beautiful underground caves, spanning an area of 3200 square meters. After heavy rainfall underground rivers come to the surface in the forest of Ses Fonts Ufanes like flat geysers, causing fast-flowing torrents.

Tests of sediment and underground water flows have revealed that the Balearic Islands are linked to the Pyrenees Mountains by deep rivulets running beneath the Mediterranean Sea.

The Cathedral of Santiago de Compostela is undoubtedly Spain's spiritual center, dating far back to the pre-Christian Celtic and Roman eras.

The steep, green mountains of Galicia that arise from the river valleys have inspired singers, poets and spiritual seekers throughout the ages.

The hill where the casket containing the remains of St. James was found and where the Cathedral of Santiago was later built was probably a religious site in pre-Christian times.

Walking into Santiago from Mount Gozo, the medieval pilgrim immediately saw the cathedral as a focal point rising from the morning fog. One can only imagine the feelings upon arriving at the destination after an arduous walk lasting several months. Today that view is sadly obscured by several modern high-rise buildings.

Maps of medieval towns show how mindfully our ancestors went about planning their cities. The place of worship was always built on the highest plateau or center, with all the other buildings in circular form around it. Shamans and geomancers were consulted so that the buildings conformed to the harmony principles of the universe.

We seem to have lost something elementary in sacrificing so much on the altar of materialism.

The coastal route of the Camino Portuguese passes through the beautiful Spanish town of Pontevedra, which has started an experiment by banning the car from the city center. More cars used to pass through the city streets than people who lived there.

It was a city in decline, polluted, noisy, dirty and occupied by the drug scene, with those who could afford it moving out of town.

Now all of the 300,000 square meters of the medieval center has been returned to the pedestrian. Everyone in the city is walking or travelling by bicycle. The entire city can be crossed with a 25-minute walk.

The surface car parks were closed and others opened on the city periphery. Carbon dioxide emissions are down by two thirds. Deaths by traffic accidents have been reduced to zero. While other rural towns in Spain are seeing declining populations, Pontevedra has gained 12,000 new inhabitants since 2009.

The Essentials:

- How we treat ourselves is how we treat the world.
- Time spent in nature is reconnecting with the higher self and the universe.
- As we learn to be guardians at the gateway to our souls we need to be guardians of our natural environment.
- Respect the sacred places and symbols of all religions.
- Our happiness and health is dependent on where and how we live.

Chapter 21

Transformation of the Cross

I t is easy to bond with people on the Camino. You share daily experiences, memories and the highs and lows that come with a pilgrimage walk.

Then comes the time to say goodbye, which can be a painful process if you have spent days and weeks walking with someone. It is like saying goodbye to an old friend when you know it will be some time before you will see each other again.

Ray was a veteran pilgrim, walking the Camino for the last time. He had undergone surgery for colon cancer some weeks before, and was taking his walk slowly and with great mindfulness.

It was from the awareness that every moment that he still had to live was precious. "I've been on this same path many times," he confided, "but this time I am seeing so many things I did not see before."

"It is like reading a good book, and then you read it a second time

131

and a third time, discovering each time something new from a different state of awareness," he said.

Talking with Ray led to the realization that life itself is meaning and the purpose of each individual is moving to a higher state of consciousness during a lifetime whose end we cannot predict.

Ray decided to take a few days' rest near the town of Sarria, wanting to walk the last 100 kilometers (62 miles) to Santiago in his own time.

On saying goodbye, Ray gave me a Christian cross that he had lovingly carved out of wood from an olive tree.

While I was touched by his gift that came from the heart, I had mixed feelings about the cross that also symbolized the "corporate identity" of the church with which I had a long-troubled relationship.

I was unaware at the time that my pilgrim friend had given me an astounding gift. I hung it around my neck, its mystery opening to me with every step to Santiago and healing the old wound.

In the Christian tradition the cross is the symbol of Christ's pain and suffering. It resonated with the people in the Middle Ages who themselves went through a dark time of humanity. But in the modern era?

The tragedy is that the fixation on this symbol of suffering misses the essence of Jesus' teachings—that of transmuting suffering and death in resurrection.

This might sound blasphemous for some but we have a religion focused on life being an endless endurance of pain and suffering with the salvation only coming in the hereafter.

This was very much the thinking during the Middle Ages. Christians paid tithes to the church to "buy" their way into heaven. With disease, war and childbirth being a constant daily reminder that life on earth could be a short sojourn, the church fed into the fears of what comes in the afterlife. If certain beliefs, habits and rules were not followed, you ended up in the eternal flames of hell.

Life on earth at the time must surely have been hell for many people, struggling to eke out a living in the overcrowded towns and cities infested with rodents and human excrement. Living in the rural areas was no better, as every freak weather condition could mean a failed harvest and famine.

The devil was blamed for bad luck, accidents, immoral behavior, theft, illness and death. He was frequently depicted in places of worship, paintings and manuscripts of the time. Hell was a dark underground world ruled by Satan and full of demons, monstrosity and deformity. The horrors could not be worse if you turned your back against God and the church.

At the same time Christ was the savior in the sky above. Depictions of heaven and Christ could frequently be found on high ceilings and on top of the altar. God's mercy and the reward in the afterlife came after leading a life following rules and beliefs.

There are many depictions of the world of darkness and the world of light in the old cathedrals, chapels and churches on the Camino, such as in Jaca, Lugo and Oviedo, giving an inkling of the mindset of the time.

The dividing lines between good and evil could not be more vivid.

In contrast, the Cathedral of Santiago is an expression of joy. It probably stems from the joy many pilgrims felt in finally reaching their destination after months of arduous walking. The Monte de Gozo, or Mountain of Joy, is situated on a hilltop from where the pilgrims had a beautiful view of the ancient city of Santiago.

The Portal of Glory in the cathedral features over 200 Romanesque sculptures, featuring angels, saints and prophets. Angels carry and lead the soul to paradise. The angels play instruments in concert to the glory of God.

Built in the form of a cruciform, the cathedral is almost austere coming from the entrance but opens up to a magnificent organ and choir with illuminated chapels on either side.

Even today pilgrims are overwhelmed when entering the cathedral for the first time.

If he or she has walked on the northern route, he/she will have passed by numerous crosses along the wayside, depicting the crucified Christ in many shapes and forms of gruesome suffering.

No wonder the first Vikings visiting England went back to their homeland telling their people that the Anglo-Saxons were easy prey because they were worshipping a dead God.

The cross is in fact an old symbol pre-dating Christian times and deeply embedded in pagan and Celtic tradition.

In many of the churches and chapels on the Camino the "Goddess," the Virgin Mary, is the central figure on the altar. Especially in Galicia the ancient stone crosses depict Jesus on the one side and the Mother Mary on the other, which on a symbolic level unites the male and the female aspect.

One of the sad aspects of the Protestant movement was the banishment of the Madonna, the female aspect, from the altar, replacing it with the crucifix.

Many priceless artifacts were burned and destroyed in the fanatic 30-year religious war between Catholicism and Protestantism that ravaged central Europe in the 15th century.

While the Roman Cross has a long central vertical line, the Celtic cross has both the vertical and horizontal lines in equal length, with a circle around it.

The horizontal lines symbolize the past and the future, with the mind locked in one of these two thoughts on a daily basis. The vertical line, however, represents the alignment with the above and the below, the awakened state of the present "heart moment" in the center where the cross meets.

We thus find many an ancient painting depicting a heart or a mandala in the center of the cross.

As we say the old Celtic powerful prayer of protection, we visualize the Goddess, the Mother, Mary, the Madonna:

She is as above me as below, to the left and to the right, before me and behind me as well as within me.

Chapter 22

Faith Over Fear

There is a deep yearning in the human mind to feel safe and secure, originating from the time we spent in our mother's womb, where we felt protected from the elements.

In contrast to most mammals we are born completely helpless, dependent and without fur to protect us from the heat and cold.

A common fear among pilgrims on the Camino is that of not finding a place to sleep after a long day of hiking. Hectic activity breaks out in the early hours of the morning in the hostels as the first hikers leave before darkness. With a determined look they take to the road, reaching the next town before midday, where they wait in line outside the hostels, which sometimes only open in the late afternoon.

People coming from the comfortable middle class with good incomes will argue over the price of a cup of coffee or why they should spend a few euros more for their accommodation.

I have often wondered why these people put themselves under so much stress at the cost of enjoying a relaxed walk in beautiful countryside and innumerable, lasting impressions.

Thousands of thoughts a day will navigate around the craving for basic needs or the fear of losing what we already have.

We need only look at divorce courts or family feuds over an inheritance to realize how much the emotion of fear is linked to money.

I've had endless discussions with family members on why I am a firm believer in making children appreciate the true value of money. This will never happen when you give every time they ask. Children need to experience boundaries with a no. We have raised a generation of children who feel entitled. I get quite annoyed at friends when they tell me how dependent their adult children still are on them financially.

The thought that money will solve the problem is an illusion. It will only delay the problem that really needs to be addressed. This is why lottery millionaires sometimes end up falling back into poverty or people who have inherited a fortune squander it all.

Buying away fear with money will never transmute the fear of loss. I've been in situations where I didn't know how to buy food for the next day. I know how deep that fear is. But the more we allow that demon to take hold, the more likely the portending fear of loss will become a reality.

Replacing the negative mantra of fear and going into the positive mantra of trusting in the caring power of the universe is the blessing that needs to be learned.

We lose everything including our body when we die. Fear of death, the concept of death and the inability to deal with mortality causes much mental stress.

Fear forces us to stay in the comfort zone. Great things never happened from the comfort zone.

Only by accepting and facing our fears as part of our shadow can we transmute those fears into courage.

Without fear there cannot be courage. It is part of the yin and yang, or the polarity of life. There is a saying that we fail to hear the whisper from the universe when we fall into procrastination and the belief that everything is running smoothly and nothing can go wrong.

But when we are hit in succession by events out of our control, we are forced to look more closely at those submerged fears we thought we had overcome.

At the age of 23, I was forced to leave my home country of South Africa to avoid three months of combat duty in what was then called the "operational area" along the Namibian-Angolan border. Almost hidden from the outside world, South Africa was involved in the largest war since Vietnam. All white men were forced into a two-year military service after schooling, followed by regular one- or three-month military stints every year after that. Refusing such a military call-up was harshly punished with a prison term that often amounted to double the time of the call-up period.

It was my first major life lesson in going into trust. I left South Africa on a container ship that arrived on a cold, snowy day in the German port city of Hamburg on January 8, 1981.

I felt completely alone and lost. I knew nobody and had little more than 20 German marks (12 dollars) in my pocket. A seaman on board the ship kindly offered to let me stay in his apartment for a couple of nights.

Would it have been better to have stayed in South Africa and fought in a war that I was opposed to? Germany was the country of my great-grand-father who emigrated to South Africa as a missionary, but I knew absolutely nobody in what was for me a completely foreign country.

Then the miracle began. A complete stranger on a ferry gave me 50 marks (29 dollars), which enabled me to buy a train ticket to my next destination, where I could stay initially with friends of friends. Despite major obstacles in getting a residence and employment permit, every-thing eventually fell into place. I eventually found a good job with an international news agency, where I worked for more than 20 years.

Then the digital revolution hit the media industry. Thousands of people lost their jobs in a once-booming newspaper sector. I had to reinvent myself from the comfort zone of what I thought was a safe job to the uncertainty of being self-employed.

So often in the first years of running my own business I did not know how to pay the bills when suddenly—literally at the last minute—the tide turned.

Two relationships in succession collapsed. I gave up my home of 21 years, dumped nearly all my possessions and moved to the island of Majorca with my dog and a few personal belongings.

Then, within the space of only a few months, my younger brother died unexpectedly and I lost three good friends to cancer.

It is in those moments of walking through the dark valley, the pit of darkness and despair, that I also felt closest the comforting hand of God—the whisper that faith and trust are always more powerful than fear. Sometimes you have to enter the darkness of doubt and fear to find the light, and to find God. It is when we go into the total and unconditional surrender, into humility, that we touch the other dimension.

Ann, a young woman in her early twenties, confided to me on the Camino that she was mortally afraid of walking alone in a foreign country. Her parents, boyfriend and all her friends tried to dissuade her from travelling.

"Do you know what it means to walk alone as a woman in a strange country? You are a man; you wouldn't know," she said.

I could relate because they were the same voices that many years ago had tried to convince me against leaving South Africa.

She had only a small budget and the challenge of dealing with the aftereffects of medication from a recent illness. But a voice inside her had turned from a whisper to an inner scream:

"You just have to do this."

Days before her trip she had sleepless nights, breaking into a cold sweat, hearing the echo of all the voices of doubt and fear from her friends and family.

She found little solace in the images of God from her childhood, a punishing God reading out the list of sins from a long scroll at the Gate of Purgatory, or a Jesus nailed to the cross.

But only a day into her walk all those fears evaporated as though they had never existed. Spain is one of those countries where women can still feel relatively safe, especially on the Camino.

A young woman with an uncertain and fearful walk had walked through her fear into strident self-confidence.

So often the fear demons of our imagination become so big that they drive us into paralysis. The truth is that those fears seldom if ever materialize in the form imagined. They are thoughts and illusions.

Resistance will always show itself when you decide to follow a dream in moving to a higher level of your consciousness. It's a natural force of the opposite that is part of the pull between yin and yang.

It is that wall between the old self and moving to the level of the self of becoming who you really are.

The resistance often comes with those inner voices that center around the sense of self-worth: "I'm not good enough. I'm not fit enough. I'm past that age. Why should I do that; it's nothing new?"

Interestingly, these voices of resistance begin to fade when you take the first steps of action. That could be painting a vision board outlining your dream, taking the first ten-minute walk for your preparation for the walk on the Camino, and learning those first few phrases of a new language.

It is that point where the pain of procrastination is greater than actually taking the first steps of "just doing it."

Fear becomes so overwhelming that you go into a state of panic. Resistance forces you to the floor into that state of utter despair and frustration. That is the point where you confront that fear and resistance directly, looking the fiery dragon in the face.

Facing and accepting fear and resistance at that low point is often the turnaround that makes you move forward. That space is often found in those moments of silence during meditation, when the buzz of thoughts stops and the ego surrenders toward acceptance.

The Essentials:

- There is no courage without fear.
- Faith over Fear and Trust over Fear.
- Accept the fear and then move forward.
- Fear begins with a thought.
- Fear forces us to stay in the comfort zone.
- The magic starts outside the comfort zone.
- Resistance is the natural opposite when following your dream.
- Just do it. Resistance fades when you take the first steps of action.

Chapter 23
Dream Dimension

O ur dreams tell us exactly at what place we are emotionally. It could be unresolved issues from the past, hidden fears, anger or sadness. It could also be the universe whispering to us.

I've had some of my most profound dreams during or in the weeks after walking the Camino, and many pilgrims have had a similar experience.

Events I thought I had dealt with years ago suddenly resurfaced in a different, very healing perspective. Even as a young child I had problems imagining God as a man with a long white beard, sternly admonishing the child for every misdemeanor. It was a long road from a constrained, intolerant religion to experiential spirituality. The female aspect of God in the form of Mary never played a role in my Protestant upbringing.

The ancient peoples in the Iberian peninsula had a strong belief that the Mother Goddess revealed herself in different shapes and forms with a specific message for individuals and for mankind as a whole at crucial junctures in life.

In most churches the altar is dominated by the figure of Jesus nailed to the cross. In the many chapels and churches along the Camino in Spain the Madonna forms the focal point, either alone or holding the baby Jesus in her arms.

Pre-Christian Goddesses, especially Isis, were often replaced with the Black Madonna. Sometimes the statues were simply renamed and old Greek and Roman temples turned into Christian churches.

In Galicia it is common for the crosses along the Camino to represent both the male and the female aspect, with Jesus nailed to one side of the cross and Mary leaning on the opposite side.

I made a particular point on one of my walks to meditate before each statue or altar of the Madonna I encountered along the way. The images had numerous facets: Sometimes she was in deep suffering, sad, serenely beautiful, expressing unconditional love to her child or in deep prayer.

In a half-sleep I woke with a start from a lucid dream where she appeared to change from statue to human form that was almost uncannily real.

I found myself in a dome of light that was more a temple than a church, with four strong rays of light coming from a skylight window and a voice telling me to concentrate and to keep my mind focused on the endless stream of consciousness.

An incident I wrote about in my fiction novel *Walking on Edge: A Pilgrimage to Santiago* was a dream recollected by a fellow pilgrim on the Camino Aragonese.

We had been walking together for some days when she had a dream, closely resembling the burning bush in the narrative from Exodus 3 of the Old Testament, when God called to Moses from a burning bush.

Moses noticed that although the fire came from the bush it was not burning.

"Do not come any closer," God said. "Take off your sandals, for the place where you are standing is holy ground." Then he said, "I am the God of your father, the God of Abraham, the God of Isaac and the God of Jacob." At this, Moses hid his face, because he was afraid to look at God."

In her dream the voice from the burning bush said:

"Please respect the Path for this is a Holy Path."

It was a clear reference to the Camino we were walking. We had been exchanging in the days prior our thoughts on those pilgrims who had walked the same path we had been walking centuries ago. At the same time we were saddened by the mindlessness with which walkers—I will not call them pilgrims—were leaving plastic bottles and other rubbish on the path.

The biblical dream of the burning bush is deeply embedded in the collective unconscious mind of the major cultures, with deeper meaning on many levels.

Fire has the power of destroying the old and cleansing the ground to make way for new growth. On a psychological level there is a necessity to burn the inhibiting demons of the past in order to open the gateway to a raised consciousness.

Many of the world's great inventors throughout the centuries made their discoveries in dreams. Albert Einstein allegedly got the clue for his theory of relativity in a dream of seeing cows jumping away from an electric fence switched on by the farmer.

Einstein saw all the cows jump away at the same time, while the farmer standing on the opposite end saw them jump away one at a time. After ruminating on the problem, Einstein concluded that events look different depending on what perspective you are looking at them from because of the time it takes for the light to reach the eyes.

The chemical benzene revolutionized production of most things we use today. Scientists had tried for years to crack the molecular code until Friedrich August Kekule von Stradonitz had an afternoon nap in which he dreamed of snakes surrounding him in shapes of hexagons, which he realized was the shape of the benzene molecule.

The father of quantum mechanics, Niels Bohr, often spoke of the inspirational dream that led to his discovery of the structure of the atom. In a dream he saw the nucleus of the atom with electrons spinning around it in much the same way as planets circle around the sun.

One of the pioneers of modern psychiatry, Carl Gustav Jung, studied dreams extensively, believing that dreams had a meaning on the story, archetypal and collective levels. If studied more closely they were capable of unlocking the wisdom of the unconscious mind.

Jung was undoubtedly one of the 20th century's most brilliant minds, having the capacity to analyze patterns of collective human thought and behavior across generational and cultural boundaries.

He once wrote to a friend about the crucial role of dreams: "You tell me you have had many dreams lately but have been too busy with your writing to pay attention to them. You have got it the wrong way around. Your writing can wait but your dreams cannot because they come unsolicited from within and point urgently to the way you must go."

Jung believed that the loss of direction, the "loss of soul," was one of the greatest tragedies to befall modern man and the main cause of private and collective derangement.

Jung was asked in a 1959 interview with the BBC's John Freeman whether he believed in God. Jung paused a moment, saying, "That is difficult to answer…I don't need to believe. I know."

Just before his death Jung wrote to his friend Sir Laurens van der Post, "I cannot define for you what God is. I can only say that my work has proved empirically that the pattern of God exists in every man, and that this pattern has at its disposal the greatest of all energies for transformation and transfiguration of his natural being. Not only the meaning of his life but his renewal and that of his institutions depend on his conscious relationship with this pattern in his collective unconscious."

The lack of purpose and a sense of meaninglessness pervade our societies. Ancient man was naturally spiritual and connected to soul, the dream world and the natural environment.

A German Christian missionary who went to South Africa in the 1960s with the intention of converting "heathen primitive people" had an epiphany when he had a conversation with an old Zulu chieftain. The missionary told the Zulu man that he had come to Africa to spread the message of God. The Zulu man looked at the missionary, somewhat confused.

"You are telling me there are people who do not believe in God. How can there be people who do not believe in a God?"

For so-called "primitive man" God was never part of a religion but fundamentally an "experience" lived every day in harmony with the natural surroundings and observance of the interaction of all living beings in the bigger matrix of things.

Mental and physical exhaustion in the form of depression is pervasive and has reached almost epidemic proportions in the modern world.

I have found that walking alone in nature is a magnificent way of training the mind by re-calibrating the senses to the world around us. The whisper of creation can be sensed by a bird song, the rustling of leaves in an ancient tree, or the clouds enveloping a mountaintop.

Most people in today's world, however, are forced to live in crowded cities that are dehumanizing in their detachment from nature. They cloud the senses with a high level of noise, pollution and bombardment of the senses. The modern human being has become so detached from his natural environment that it is causing havoc to his emotional stability.

We are bombarded constantly with the messages that tell us: "Buy this and you will be happy. Do this and you will get rich. Do this to live like a superstar. Dress like this and act like that to be loved and validated by the crowd."

Along the way one of our most valuable assets—the time to be fully aware of the moment—is getting lost. The mind is constantly occupied with either the past or the fears of the future. In the process of the game you can easily forget who you really are.

Keeping a dream diary and specifically writing down the feeling, that first emotion on waking up from that dream, I have found to be particularly helpful at key points in my life.

The dreams will be of greater clarity if you avoid media such as late-night thriller movies on TV, Internet surfing and other electronic media. Incorporate a positive ritual like the "happy moments of the day," a prayer or five gratitudes before you go to sleep.

Dreams are a way of dealing with trauma and can be a crucial anchor in a world becoming increasingly confusing, giving a glimmer of hope and connection to soul and purpose.

The Essentials:

- Dreams are the window to your soul.
- Keep a diary of your dreams, especially of the feelings and emotions instantly after waking up. What patterns can you see in your dreams over a longer period of time?
- Avoid electronic media before going to sleep.
- Dreams have an individual, collective and subconscious meaning.

Chapter 24

Becoming into Happiness

About five years ago several top companies noted a sudden spike in the rate of long-term absenteeism. Key staff members, including project managers, were put out of action for months with a burnout, and in some cases vital operations had to be scaled down.

With business seriously affected, executives were becoming very concerned. I was one of several consultants who did on-site analysis on the reasons behind the rising number of psychological illnesses affecting employees.

Burnout is not really an illness but can be described as a state of complete emotional and physical exhaustion, closely resembling depression.

In some cases, those affected are unable to even perform mundane tasks like doing the grocery shopping or driving the kids to school. Every task becomes an unsurmountable burden. In one extreme case a supervisor was unable to touch the keyboard of her computer. Fellow workers were themselves so stressed that for days nobody even noticed that the supervisor was in urgent need of medical assistance.

Each case, of course, is different but after conducting numerous workshops on the issue and spending much time researching psychological stress factors at the workplace, I've found several common denominators.

Many of the issues have been touched on in this book, but because most people earn a living as an employee or working in a business enterprise for others, I feel the need to delve into some of the issues.

Like the city environments we live in with our detachment from nature, many a workplace has become dehumanized, with standardized production and management procedures, completely ignoring basic human needs.

Work procedures in the big corporations are standardized globally, leaving little room for individual creativity and cultural differences. People with few or no social skills, who lack even the most rudimentary traits needed in motivating and creating winning teams, are appointed as leaders.

Office space has become increasingly functional, sometimes with hundreds of people working on one floor space, one desk behind the other, leaving little room for privacy and giving employees the feeling that they are being monitored 24-7, which is true in many cases.

In a dysfunctional institution personal values and aspirations of the employees are often in conflict with the primary objectives of the establishment.

It's a major human need to leave a positive footprint, to make an impact and both to improve personal lives and to make the world a better place for children and grandchildren.

Within our own life we live the life of our time. Every generation has a major challenge. For the Baby Boomers born in the 1950s and early 1960s, it is the overcoming of ideologies, all the "isms" we were brought up with—capitalism, communism, nationalism...

For the Millennials born between 1981-1996, environmental issues are the major concern. Nearly half of the Millennials who participated in the World Economic Forum's Global Shapers Survey in 2017 believe climate change is the most serious issue affecting the world today. They came of age in a vast expansion of digital technology with all its challenges.

In the early part of my career I was a passionate journalist, having done on-site reporting on some of the world's greatest historical events such as the fall of the Iron Curtain and South Africa's transition from an apartheid state to a democracy led by Nelson Mandela.

But jobs change and the Internet triggered major structural changes in the media industry. For a while I had been deluding myself that I was still doing journalism by regurgitating news in a news factory. I had lost all sense of purpose in my job and it showed in lack of motivation and bouts of serious exhaustion. If you are doing something you don't like your whole being and higher self will start going into rebellion.

On the brink of a burnout, I took my first walk on the Camino in Spain, and that marked the beginning of a complete change in my life.

Interestingly I met a lot of people on the Camino with a similar biography: bankers in top positions who left their job because they could no longer in good conscience sell certain products to their customers; an executive in a car factory leaving shortly before a promotion because the pressure was just getting too much, and he had no more time to spend with his family; the medical doctor, who once started his career with the passion of healing other people, but had to process between 50 and 60 patients a day just to make ends meet, leaving little time to have a decent healing conversation; the teacher, who once burned with the passion of teaching a new generation the gems of English literature, but found he had to spend most of the time disciplining his class or dealing with difficult parents.

A lot of people are very unhappy in the jobs where they spend most of their precious "life-time" because the passion and energy they once had for what they were doing has been extinguished. So how do I find a way out if I have to pay for groceries and the mortgage?

It is sad to see so many people stuck in a very uncomfortable comfort groove because the fear of the unknown is preventing them from even looking at alternatives.

What I have found is that if we face up to the fear and place full trust in the universe that we are here on earth for a purpose, then the universe will respond in kind.

It is in becoming our true self that we discover the sense of meaning and belonging. We are here to develop and grow our consciousness—to become aware of the greater reality. It is part of what the evolutionary program demands of us.

Project yourself ahead in a time machine where you see yourself rocking in an armchair well into your 80s, looking back on your life. What are your greatest regrets? What are the chances missed? Probably the greatest sin would have been a life passed without even attempting the greatest dreams and following the true destiny. If only I had…

Going the route of constant self-development, self-reflection and spiritual growth is immensely rewarding. It is one of the keys to living a purposeful and happy life.

But you will never discover your true calling if you don't slow down, so that you can listen to the whisperings of the soul.

Body and mind have an infinite capacity for change and renewal. It is never too late. All the skin in the body is replaced every two to three weeks. The liver renews itself at least once every couple of years and the skeleton once every ten years.

But trauma and toxic emotions can hold us captive for decades, preventing us from moving forward and "becoming" our true self.

Stress and fear start with a thought. But the solution to a problem has never come from running thoughts and monkeys in the head. These are dark imaginary creations of the mind. Yet the mind has enormous power to create in every direction.

Thought discipline can be practiced. It is normal for negative thoughts, old anger and fears to surface when we walk alone. Replacing that dark thought with a positive thought such as gratitude is the first step in the right direction.

With gratitude comes the wisdom that in the bigger picture there is grace—the grace that we are part of a bigger matrix, that everything has meaning, that we are born to learn, grow, and to become.

The Essentials:

- Are you passionate about your work and do you have the feeling of doing something meaningful that is in alignment with your values?
- What would you change now if you saw yourself at the age of 85 and looked back on your life?
- Never stop learning! Self-development, self-reflection and spiritual growth are key to becoming your true self and living a purposeful and happy life.
- Everything starts with a thought.

Chapter 25

The Best View Comes After the Hardest Climb

O ne of the world's wealthiest men, Warren Buffet, once said, "The chains of habit are too light to be felt until they are too heavy to be broken."

One of the worst chains of physical and mental habit is procrastination. Without action there is no result.

We can dream, hope and think our wishes will come true but they will only remain dreams if they are not followed up by action.

The pain of breaking the chains of habit is perceived as greater than the pain and the fear of facing an uncertain future. It is the reason we stay in dysfunctional relationships, fail to change an unfulfilling job and refuse to change a diet that is ruining our health.

A few kilometers away from my home on the island of Majorca, a path leads up the Tramuntana Mountains to the monastery of Lluc. A new route on the Camino starts from the monastery, taking the pilgrim across the island. A ferry has to be taken to the mainland at Porto Alcudia to Barcelona, where the path continues across Catalonia to Jaca, where it joins the Camino Aragonese, which in turn leads to the main Camino Frances in Puenta la Reina.

Until only a few decades ago it was common for pilgrims to creep for eleven kilometers on their knees from the village of Caimari on a path strewn with sharp stones and rocks to seek penance from the Black Madonna of Lluc.

The sandstone sculpture of the Madonna is an impressive masterpiece on an altar in the monastery chapel. Once the pilgrims reached the hilltop Refugi Son Amer hostel, they were offered the stupendous view of the monastery complex in the valley below.

According to legend the Madonna was found by a Muslim shepherd named Lluc in a cave in the area shortly after the Christian conquest of the island in 1229. It was brought the same day to the local parish in nearby Escorca.

When the inhabitants came the next day to worship the Madonna she had disappeared, only to be found again near the stream where she was originally discovered.

The incident repeated itself the next day, whereupon the local priest decided that a chapel and adjacent monastery would be built at the spot.

It is a common theme in several parts of the Camino for the Black Madonna to disappear from places where church authorities wanted to place her, always returning to the natural spot where she was found— harking back to the Goddess of pre-Christian times with her close association to magical places in nature.

If you look at the mountaintop before starting your walk you might well lose all your willpower. Walking the Arles route over Somport to Jaca takes the hiker up an elevation of 1632 meters.

It can be daunting, especially during bad weather in the Pyrenees and carrying a heavy backpack. Yet I have seen people of relatively frail stature manage the path up to Somport, which offers a spectacular view of the Spanish and French countryside below.

I started my 26-kilometer (16.15 mile) walk on the Hospitales Route of the Camino Primitivo on a foggy, overcast morning. I had slept badly in the hostel near the hamlet of Borres. Several snoring pilgrims had kept me awake for most of the night and the air in the crowded room shared with several other people smelt of cooked food and smelly socks.

After such a night, I was in a grumpy mood, asking myself why I was doing all this.

The path snakes up a mountain ridge to an elevation of 1264 meters. It is called the Hospital Route because in ancient times nuns ran a hospital for pilgrims on the mountain peak. Supplies were transported from the hamlets below with mules.

After slipping and sliding along the muddy path for a good two hours, I turned a corner when suddenly the sky opened in all its magnificence. The view of the cloud-covered Asturian countryside below was stunning. These are the moments of the Camino I have frozen in memory.

It was a moment of gratitude when all else faded into insignificance—a breathtaking view from above.

Apart from the bees humming and the echo of cow bells, there was absolute silence and complete appreciation of the moment. I felt a magical, vibrant thrust of energy in my body that carried me forward with a lightness of being that I cannot explain until this day.

So often when we are on the brink of giving up in walking through that long, dark tunnel of obstacles, the breakthrough comes in the most unexpected moment.

It is almost as if the universe is testing our willpower, creativity and clarity of thought on the walk through life.

The yin and yang, the law of opposites, is an active process of life force, "qi" energy, swinging us from one extreme to the next in the never-ending cycle of growth and change.

The first light of dawn can only be seen in the darkness. Deep happiness is a feeling that is all the more intense after we have gone through the experience of sadness. They are both intense feelings. There is a fine line between love and hate, as William Shakespeare vividly portrays in "Romeo and Juliet."

The moral of the story is that nothing good can come from blindly embracing fully the one or the other.

In Act 1 Scene 1, Romeo is well aware of the close relationship between these two strong emotions:

"Here's much to do with hate, but more with love.
Why then, O brawling love, O loving hate,
O anything of nothing first create!
O heavy lightness, serious vanity,
Misshapen chaos of well-seeming forms,
Feather of lead, bright smoke, cold fire, sick health,
Still-waking sleep, that is not what it is!
This love feel I, that feel no love in this."

When we fall in love we tend to see the other in a rose-colored hue of positivity. Love appears all-encompassing and we are blind to character traits or habits that are difficult to reconcile.

The disappointment comes later, when we move in with each other and the fights start over who is responsible for the grocery shopping or cleaning the bathroom. Shattered hopes and dreams of what an idealized relationship never was or could have been is one of the main reasons for the breakup of so many relationships.

Much of the animosity in the political divide comes from the same energy—embracing either the right or the left of the spectrum without seeing the nuances in between. The one is the shadow of the other. Both extremes have a shocking level of intolerance and are rooted in fundamentalism that prevents them from listening to each other.

Especially in the United States the pendulum in elections swings from one side to the other, with the nation almost equally divided between the two extremes.

The challenge in the law of opposites is finding the middle ground—that difficult territory where the truth has many shades of gray.

The tendency toward extremist positions is rooted in uncertainty and fear from lack of grounding.

The Chinese masters placed great emphasis on this aspect—not only as crucial in the martial arts but as a life philosophy.

Without a solid foundation in dealing with the mundane, any type of self-development will come to naught.

The ancient Jewish sages went further in teaching that if we fail to master the normal daily activities such as looking after our health, family relationships and livelihood, we cannot hope to advance to higher spiritual experience.

Thus, a good portion of life in the monastery is spent in cleaning, gardening and other menial chores. It is not only a practice in humility but stems from the knowledge that mastering the mundane is the gateway to loftier spheres.

In apartheid South Africa it was common for black domestic servants to perform all menial tasks for their white employers. My grandmother insisted, however, that we children learn from an early age the necessity of helping in the household and doing our share in the garden—sometimes much to our dismay.

In retrospect it was a good thing, for the evil ideology of apartheid also very much enslaved the white perpetrators.

Physical exercise and the mindful carrying out of mundane chores are excellent for grounding. If your work is mostly in a sitting position in an office, it is crucial to use breaks for walking or other exercises.

The "Yoga tree posture" is especially effective as a grounding morning exercise.

- Fold your hands with the forefingers touching each other.
- Ground yourself with your right foot, imagining roots like those of a tree growing from the center of your foot deep into the earth.
- Place your left foot at the height of your right knee and then lift your hands with forefingers pointed to the sky above the focal point of your skull.
- Imagine that you are mentally connected by a stream of energy to the sky above your head and the earth below your foot.
- Repeat the exercise with the left foot.
- You can close the exercise with a powerful mantra or prayer aligning all your activities of the day with what God, the universe or any other deity has planned for you that day.

In a meditation sequence you can imagine yourself walking up a steep mountain. Reaching the top, you inhale with the mantra:

- I am a big mountain.

Exhaling, you say the words:

- I feel your powerful grounding energy throughout my body.

The Essentials:

- Without action there is no result.
- The reward comes only after a hard climb.
- Mastering the mundane is the gateway to higher spiritual experience.
- The breakthrough often comes in the moments of our deepest despair.
- The challenge in the law of opposites is in finding the middle ground.

Chapter 26

Living a Life of Bliss

Three weeks of walking on the Camino, then I feel that moment of total bliss on a beautiful afternoon in the luscious green mountains of Galicia.

It is that moment of "runners' high" in feeling that empty space within and beyond the body. I've known that same feeling after long practice of yoga or tai chi, where the body is in total synchronicity with the movement.

Every step comes easy, like the body is floating on a woolen carpet and is pulled along a string by some invisible, gentle force.

It comes after days of walking through a tunnel of aches and pains, countless thoughts racing through the mind and a topsy-turvy whirlwind of emotions.

The tunnel is going through that necessary phase of detox before body and mind can proceed with rebirth and renewal.

159

After numerous conversations on the Camino with people from all walks of life, different nations and age groups, a common denominator seems to be the search for meaning and purpose after hitting a wall in a relationship, career or being confronted with a serious health issue.

There comes a defining moment or "midlife crisis" where the question arises: "How much time do I have left to do the things I need to do?"

A parent expects a child to become a lawyer or a doctor because they would be "safe" earning a good salary. A young woman is expected to surrender her inner calling by getting married and having children.

You start counting the years and the months left until retirement so that you can then "finally start living and doing the things you always wanted to do."

Karl was one of these guys who could easily afford a comfortable hotel room on the Camino but chose instead to sleep in a bunk bed of an albergue like all the other pilgrims.

He enjoyed the company and the conversations in the evening. "Much better than being all alone in a hotel room," he said.

Karl was in recuperation after suffering a burnout—that state of total emotional and physical exhaustion that comes after years of continuous daily stress.

He was the chief doctor of a medical clinic in Germany, faced with constant restructuring, cost-cutting and other measures after the hospital was turned from a state-owned institution into a privately-run facility.

From our conversation it emerged that he had simply done what was expected of him in the family tradition, his father and grandfather having been medical doctors.

He must have excelled at his job to have obtained a position as a chief doctor, yet he was at a turning point in his life, knowing that something had to change fundamentally to preserve his mental and physical well-being. He was simply unhappy with what he was doing.

I never saw Karl again after our conversation that evening, and hopefully he found answers for himself on the Camino.

A large portion of people in today's modern workforce are unhappy.

Work procedures are heavily standardized and constrained, giving little opportunity for the individual to express his/her own ideas and creative mind. Personal values are often in conflict with the day-to-day realities of the workplace.

The term "Human Resources" for the staff management department is a telling example of how far the treatment of human beings in corporate structures has degenerated.

The rebellion is showing in a growing number of the employed withdrawing into a "silent misery" in doing only what is necessary, counting the days to the next vacation and the years to retirement. When the day finally comes most of the precious retirement funds are spent visiting doctors and attending to bodily ailments.

Too many people in my former work environment literally fell into a dark hole of procrastination and serious illness and death only a few years into retirement.

It happens also to people where the rug is pulled from under their feet in retrenchment and restructuring when they are forced to leave the "comfort zone" of what was a supposedly safe job.

Life is full of unexpected turns and twists and the unexpected collapse of a well-planned career path can throw people completely off balance.

Nobody would have thought two decades ago that digital technology and robotics would destroy hundreds of thousands of jobs in industry and manufacturing and at the same time create completely new avenues of income.

Age-old institutions like marriage are very much in crisis. Divorce statistics are indicative of a major shift in relationships.

The combination of problems at work and relationship problems at home is very often the reason for a burnout. Body and mind shut down when it all becomes too much to carry.

Remaining in a comfort zone will blind you to the storm clouds rising on the horizon. When you realize that it's time to take action, it will be too late. The storm will run you over. It is the unwritten code that determines the survival of all life forms.

Only a few people have learned to weather any unexpected catastrophe in their lives by placing their center in the heart and aligning with heaven and earth.

An organism has the flexibility to adapt to changes in its habitat, changing its response or moving to a different environment. The species that fails to adapt to the continuous changes of the wheel of life will inevitably be doomed.

The natural response of most humans in an economic environment of major change is to blame management, the government, foreigners or other external factors.

It is the fear of the unknown that prevents most people from taking action when the writing is all over the wall.

Life appears easy in the comfort zone but a comfort zone over time can get very uncomfortable. Expectations are in line with what is expected. But there is no magic left in the air.

One of the world's most successful entrepreneurs, Richard Branson, once summed it up like this:

"I can honestly say that nothing good in my life has ever happened from the safety of my comfort zone. It's all those moments where you feel challenged, where you think 'Oh crap, maybe this wasn't such a good idea' and then ponder giving up—if you can get through this stage of doubt and make it out the other side—I promise you, this is where the good stuff happens."

Staying with the mundane and with the routine is the reason so many people lose their drive and enthusiasm in the jobs they do.

It is also the reason so many marriages end in divorce. The degeneration of a loving, romantic relationship does not happen overnight.

After a period of time the realization sets in that falling in love is just not enough and is unsustainable if the partners don't have a shared vision and values and some form of shared life philosophy.

A mature marriage is one where each partner supports the other in growing to become their full self. If there is no individual development taking place then something is out of balance.

The imbalance is when there is competition when the masculine or the feminine takes over control. The woman loses her femininity and the man his masculinity.

In mythology and literature marriage and love often seem to contradict each other. Love was romanticized in the Renaissance but arranged marriages were common practice until the 18th century. They are still common in some religions and cultures like those in India.

At least in Western culture today the institution of marriage as a lifelong partnership is very much showing signs of decay. Traditional roles where the man is free to follow the path of achievement while the woman tends to home and family are no longer valid.

It is sad to see when one or both partners in a marriage are obviously unhappy with each other but are in some way dependent on each other. I observed a couple on a three-hour flight not exchanging a single word, sitting next to each other in morose silence.

Communication is dead when a husband and wife with their two children spend the entire evening in a fancy restaurant, hardly aware of the food they are eating while their attention is focused on their smart phones.

Couples stay together only out of financial necessity or because leaving would be too uncomfortable and disruptive.

We are social beings and need face-to-face communication as part of our social skill set and affirming relationship. Inter-human communication cannot be replaced by a smart phone. We miss out on all the other things like tone of voice, facial expression and the aura of the other person.

We are in the early stage of an unusual human experiment where for the first time technology is having a major impact on our inter-human relationships and social skill set.

It is a huge unknown what social skill set young children of today will have as adults if they spend most of their formative years glued to a game on a smart phone.

A life of bliss is hard work in following habits of life transformation that include all areas of the wheel of life on a daily basis. These are work, family-leisure time, relationships, finances, hobbies, spiritual growth and development, home environment and health.

If work pressures and stress consume so much energy that other life areas are neglected, you will be unhappy. In turn, if you have a fulfilling job that does not pay your rent or your groceries, you won't be happy either. Or if your private relationships are in a mess, this will reflect on your performance at your workplace.

A life of bliss is very possible. We are only to a limited extent children of fate. We have freedom of choice but we are too often imprisoned by bad habits and avoid decisions because we fear the unknown.

It takes effort and action to get up earlier every morning for a meditation and exercise routine. But the long-term effects on health and mindset are astounding.

Feed the mind with quality information. We can choose to avoid the distraction of a TV soap and to replace it with self-development audios, a good book or a creative hobby.

A positive mindset and thought control require as much training as every other discipline.

Follow your bliss, do what you love, do what triggers your enthusiasm and the truth within you.

The Essentials:
- Have you placed your ladder against the wrong wall?
- Find out what triggers your enthusiasm and everything else will follow.
- Happiness is a choice and comes only when all areas of life are in balance.
- Face-to-face communication is essential for a social skill set, honing emotional intelligence or EQ.

Chapter 27

Healing Relationships

Leaving an albergue at sunrise one morning, I ran across a middle-aged Austrian couple having a heated argument over where to go at a crossroads.

The end result was that the husband walked off in a huff in one direction while the wife took the other path.

I met them again some days later at the airport in Santiago, sitting in morose silence next to each other.

The husband confided to me that his "strong-willed" wife had decided to take the "wrong way" and that they had finally only found each other again at the airport.

I've seen many couples walk the Camino together, and it has its challenges. If there is no clarity on different needs and expectations, the walk can become a nightmare.

The simple test is to compare the five greatest needs. If the three foremost needs aren't in synchronicity then those are the red flags going up in a massive way.

I've experienced numerous pilgrims walking off trauma from divorces and broken relationships, some going back many years. It is always amazing how many people are kept captive by wounds from the past that become obsessive in nature.

Undoubtedly a happy partnership and marriage are key to leading a life of bliss. Everyone who has gone through a divorce will agree that along with the death of a close family member, it is one of the most traumatic events in life.

Marriage is in crisis, like so many of our institutions. Only a generation ago divorce was taboo and those affected were socially ostracized. Today multiple divorces and patchwork families have become the norm, with all the associated complex human interactions and emotional baggage that comes with it.

Falling in love is simply not enough. If there is no shared vision and philosophy on fundamental aspects of life, estrangement is inevitable. Once the romantic stage of a partnership starts moving into the reality of a shared life together, differences that were blurred by sexual attraction and romantic love burst to the fore.

It is common for couples to go into the blame game by blaming the other for old emotional pain that sometimes has its roots in a childhood trauma.

The question is what did we fall in love with? We reenact subconsciously the partnership patterns, including all the drama and shadow aspects we know from our parents.

Marriage is either a contract or a spiritual covenant. People meet and fall in love because they made a covenant to help each other on the path of spiritual growth.

Soul partnership can only be achieved if the shadow is transmuted. The common belief is that if we meet just the right man or woman, we will be happy.

It is a delusion to think that anybody outside ourselves can make us happy. Disappointment inevitably results when the veil falls.

The frequency you create within yourself attracts the respective partner. If you work hard on transmuting your shadow and doing soul work, you will attract the right partner.

Marriage is a yielding of the individual to a relationship, discovering and fulfilling the needs of the other while making the partner understand one's own needs. It is an interplay of the yin and yang.

I've seen many couples on the Camino fall into the typical drama trap. The husband withdraws, feeling the need to walk alone. The wife feels abandoned while expecting protection from her man in what she perceives to be an alien and foreign environment. With each side not communicating openly about its different needs, the conflict is predictable.

Ideally the partners support and empower each other in spiritual growth. In dysfunctional relationships one or both partners are drained emotionally. When a perceived need is not met or the shadow from an old hurt is triggered by the partner, the drama unfolds.

The breakdown in a relationship comes creeping slowly, with red flags going up everywhere but not being seen by those in the drama bubble.

We have been conditioned by religion that a marriage vow is not to be broken. However, people change and it is not uncommon for marriage partners to block each other in becoming what they are meant to be.

Partners are unwilling to listen to each other, interrupting each other in mid-sentence, or the body language telling everyone in the room, "There you go again, you old jerk."

Worse still, communication has been reduced to the mundane.

Both partners are left living in misery and barely tolerating each other, because souls are crying out for action on unfulfilled business.

Making excuses for staying together "for the children," financial reasons, or simply because of the fear of going it alone is delaying action.

Marriage is each partner surrendering to the other, giving up a previous life as an individual to live together. But when one or both partners lose each other, when compromise after compromise is made, both end up living unfulfilled lives of compromise.

Relationships are constant work and reflection on different needs and expectations. If you are hoping to clear up marriage issues on the Camino you most likely will be disappointed. If you have a loving soul partnership prior to your walk, the Camino will be an unforgettable experience where both move in synchronicity to a higher spiritual consciousness.

From my personal subjective observations on the Camino, deep bonding has occurred when mother and daughter, father and son, and grandparent and grandchild have walked together.

I've also walked with good friends where there was honesty and clarity from the beginning in respecting space and boundary.

We are part of a matrix of relationships. Who we are is determined from early childhood by our associations with the people closest to us.

"Tell me who your friends are and I'll tell you who you are." The saying was first coined by the American coach, speaker and author Jim Rohn.

Close friends and marriage partners are known to share each other's views and values, dress code and even mannerisms.

The energy frequency on which we are moving determines who we make friends with and want to spend time with.

Everything is relationship. When we are born the closest relationship is with the mother. It evolves from there to the forming of identity and self in puberty, when part of the process is rejecting everything the parental generation stands for.

But relationship has many levels of interaction. The image of self is so often colored by external influences that few people know who they really are and what their innermost needs are.

Who are you in the gigantic web of living beings on earth? What is your relationship to your physical self and the external world around you? How we treat the earth is very much a reflection on how we treat ourselves.

A loving and caring identity to self, freed from the debris of the past, reflects on nearly all our relationships, whether to a beloved one or to friends and family.

Animals are naturally bound to the universal matrix with a sixth sense, reacting extremely sensitively to changes in the environment. Historians recorded that animals including rats, snakes and weasels deserted the Greek city of Helice in 373 B.C. days before an earthquake devastated the area (*National Geographic*, Nov. 11, 2003).

Eyewitness accounts of the 2004 tsunami in Southeast Asia reported elephants moving to higher ground, dogs refusing to leave their shelters and flamingoes abandoning low-lying breeding grounds.

Dogs can pick up olfactory cues from humans (*New Scientist*, Oct. 19, 2007), even smelling emotions such as fear and aggression. Dog owners have always known this and science is increasingly proving them right.

A pilgrimage walk is very much a discovery of relationship to self, to God or the universal intelligence. Some pilgrims describe it like a walk home as awareness grows that we are not alone and that we can go into trust.

German philosopher Martin Buber in his book *Ich und Du* (translated as *I and Thou*) finds that human life essentially finds meaning and purpose in relationships.

In this view all our relationships ultimately bring us into relationship with God or our Creator.

In the Christian mystic tradition, it is about finding the God within. We are part of the creation matrix and not separate from it.

In the Gospel of St. Thomas, discovered at Nag Hammadi in Egypt in 1945, Jesus is quoted as saying:

"See, the kingdom is in the sky, then the birds of the sky will precede you. If they say to you, 'It is in the sea,' then the fish will precede you. Rather, the kingdom is inside of you, and it is outside of you. When you come to know yourselves, then you will become known, and you will realize that it is you who are the sons of the living father (**Saying 3,** p. 654.9-21).

This is closely related to the words of Greek philosopher Pythagoras: *"Man, know thyself: then thou shalt know the Universe and God."*

The Essentials:

- Compare the checklist of the five most important needs in the relationship.
- Are you getting energy from the relationship or is it draining energy from you?
- Are you in the drama cycle of triggering old emotional pain in the other?
- Are you in the position of extracting yourself from a relationship-drama by taking a step back and watching the situation from a bird's-eye perspective?
- Is the emotional shift of moving from negative to a positive energy still possible?

Chapter 28

Raised Consciousness

*The goal of life is to make your heartbeat match the beat of the
universe, to match your nature with Nature.*
– Joseph Campbell

There is an inner voice of wisdom in each one of us that is waiting
to give expression to soul-purpose. It is a voice that speaks to us
in dreams, visions, signs and unexpected synchronicities.

The lives we live are so disconnected from our natural surroundings
that it is becoming increasingly difficult to break through a barrier of
false reference points.

We are obsessed with the narcissism of celebrity culture. Hollywood
movies are designed with happy endings. There is simplistic baddy versus
goody drama. Subliminal messages tell us all the time that others are

171

172 | DEEP WALKING

doing it better and are having an easier ride.

Nobody can escape the human condition. Life can be difficult and a topsy-turvy world of ups and downs, disappointments, separations, illnesses, deaths, yet also wonderful in its mystery, adventure, love, and caring communion.

After my many walks on the Camino I truly believe in a higher intelligence that has created life. And anyone who has spent time in the African bush can observe closely the miracle of the interconnectedness of life, from the dung beetle to the elephant.

God or the higher intelligence speaks to us in dreams, symbols and sometimes through other people.

One of the most telling dreams in the history of mankind is found in the Old Testament of the Bible. Jacob, the son of Isaac and grandson of Abraham, was forced to flee from the wrath of his brother Esau. He lay down for the night when he had a dream or a vision of a ladder connecting heaven and earth, with God's angels ascending and descending on the stairway.

There are many interpretations of this dream but the most poignant seems to me one of spiritual alignment and elevation.

The ladder can be seen as symbolic for the ascending and descending stages of man in spiritual development, with the source of the ladder in heaven but rooted at the bottom to the ground. There is a strong connection between two dimensions.

Communication with God or the Universe is not a one-way street. It is a dialogue and a partnership between the creator and the created.

The dream came to Jacob as he found himself in a wasteland, in fear for his life and literally flat on the ground in hopelessness.

In that moment of darkness came reassurance from the Creator himself that he was not alone and had been chosen for a special purpose—as we all have been chosen to be born with meaning.

Some weeks after I completed the Camino Portuguese, I had a deeply spiritual dream:

I found myself in a beautiful cathedral in awe about the stained glass windows and the sacred place I found myself in. I could literally feel on a physical level the powerful inspiration of the place.

Priests led me into a courtyard, where I conversed with several of them on the differences between the theological explanation of God and the experiential experience, arguing my case that it was impossible to make people believe in something—God could only be experienced.

It seemed that this message was most upsetting for some people, even demons who appeared on a balcony above and started throwing rocks at me. As I dodged my way out, a group of nuns walked by in a procession, singing a beautiful song.

My adversaries retreated almost immediately, some of them fleeing in mortal terror. The message: A song that stirred a positive feeling could be more powerful than any weapon.

I come from a background where we children were taught to literally believe everything stated in the Bible. It is the problem between religion and spirituality. Even as a child I was questioning the theology of "you have to just believe."

Children see very quickly what is fake and what is real. The bigotry in apartheid South Africa was a very real day-to-day reality. A government was justifying racial discrimination and horrific human rights violations with the Calvinist doctrine of predestination—that the white Afrikaners were God's chosen people.

If God created everyone, how could one race be above the other one and be more privileged than the other was a question I was mulling, even in my early school years.

A child knows intuitively that a person of different race or color feels exactly the same pain as every other human being.

It was only after the fall of apartheid that the Dutch Reformed Church in South Africa, the religious backbone of apartheid, finally did come to the conclusion that apartheid was a sin.

Appearing before the Truth and Reconciliation Commission in 1997 the leader of the church Reverend Freek Swanepoel finally said, "Our hearts ache and we confess that great wrongs have been done."

The separation of humanity from its own deeper core is a question of our time. The loss of the spiritual is having a devastating effect on the mental health of our societies as the search for satisfaction in the immediate gratification of the senses becomes increasingly hollow.

A common misconception we often hear is: "If God exists why does he allow evil to happen?"

As a young reporter in South Africa I witnessed in a court two heavyweight white security policemen who were accused of torture by a black anti-apartheid politician. I felt a damp coldness in the room as I observed the darkened, cynically grinning policemen. This was looking evil in the eye.

It was the same feeling I had some months later when I covered a murder case. The man in the dock, the son of a pastor, was accused of brutally raping, mutilating and killing an innocent young girl. Again, I had the feeling of looking into the abyss of evil. The accused was later sentenced to death by hanging.

Evil is not created by God. It manifests itself where there is complete absence of God.

Man has been given freedom of choice by the creator. But that also gives him the choice between good and evil.

Zoroastrianism, created by the prophet Zoroaster between 1500 and 1000 BC in Central Asia, saw the world as a cosmic battle between the good god Ahura Mazda and the evil god Angra Mainyu, with humans given the task of helping the good god.

This dualism has been absorbed by Christianity with the evil force Satan fighting the good God.

In the dualism of yin and yang of Taoist philosophy the world is constantly pulled between these two forces. One cannot exist without the other. We define our being in comparison to the opposite.

We find the same dualism in popular culture, portrayed in the Star

Wars movies in the battle between the good forces led by Luke Skywalker and the dark forces headed by Darth Vader.

We as human beings are faced with the challenge of standing guard at the doorway to our soul. The information we feed our minds with, our immediate associations and our surroundings make us who we are.

It is easy to follow the herd, chasing after just another emotional trigger, another new dress code, fashion accessory, or new thing to have.

When observing toddlers at play, there is the little boy refusing to share his toy with a fellow child. "It's mine," he shouts.

The other boy tries to pull it away from him. "It's mine!" he screams, in a raging fit, as if his life depended on it.

Within minutes, however, the fascination with the toy is forgotten and thrown aside as the children find another object to play with.

We identify the "Self" with political and religious beliefs and the things we own. How we dress, where we live and what car we own advertise the label under which the herd identifies our status.

If someone comes with a different belief or wants to take the object away from us, we go into attack mode. These exterior trappings have little connection with the true self and higher consciousness.

In breaking through the smokescreen of what was mainly the ego-identity comes the awakening to the soul path and true identity.

But even with the rise of greater spiritual consciousness, evil will show itself in all its facets, and nobody is immune. One of Christianity's central messages is that we need to forgive because we are all imperfect human beings.

Evil is in principle always divisive and destructive—most visible where there is abuse of power. We are seeing it with the rise of xenophobia, intolerance, and greedy destruction of our natural habitat.

The shadow can lurk behind the cloak of a clergyman or in dark messages and symbols on social media, negatively affecting the subconscious mind of the innocent child.

An awakened mind starts with the awareness of what choices we make on a daily basis. What food are we eating? Was it produced by exploited farmworkers? Does the meat come from animals from a cruel mass production facility? If the animals were under stress when slaughtered we will take up those same stress hormones in our bodies.

What clothing and body lotions are we using that have both a negative impact on our body and that of the environment?

Elevation to higher consciousness comes at a point where there is deep honesty of heart and humility, yet at the same time the loving acceptance of self.

Are my personal values in alignment with my occupation and way of life? If there is a discrepancy, it will inevitably lead to an inner conflict.

Higher consciousness seeks the common thread in humanity and the pattern of God in all of creation. It is an energy that transmutes the needs of self into the needs of the larger whole. It is unconditional love and one of service to the other.

It is a belief in a God who is experiential. We cannot believe. We can only experience. The believing is external while the experiential comes from the heart of being. Experience can be communicated to the other by the limited means of language, art or song but the feeling will always remain unique and individual.

The deepest individual spiritual experience can only be sensed but never experienced by the other in the same way. It remains unique and exceptional.

Walking on ancient paths trodden by soul-seekers for hundreds of years is becoming for a growing number of people a search for that mystical spirit of the past that has become lost in an age of logic and rationalism.

It is but one of a variety of methods that can be chosen. Crucial, however, is taking a time out for yourself to reconnect.

Time has become a precious commodity. This comes, curiously, at a time in human development where we spend less time than ever in time and energy to gather food and water.

Retreat centers are opening in many places around the globe as more and more people seek guidance to higher consciousness.

Countless self-development books show a deep need for renewal and growth.

Reconnection, however, need not be in a complex meditation practice. It can be too overwhelming. Starting with simple and regular daily exercises can make a huge difference.

One of them is to find time every day to concentrate on breathing meditation. All you need to do is to sit comfortably, closing your eyes and concentrating on your natural breathing rhythm. When inhaling you count one and when exhaling you count one. You can continue until the count of 21.

When walking in nature you can deepen your experience by pausing. Find one sound in your immediate surroundings that appeals to you. It could be the rushing of water in the creek, the singing of a blackbird or the rushing of wind in the leaves of a tree. Blanket out all other sounds from your consciousness and concentrate on just that one vibration.

It is in the push against our most toxic emotions, in confronting our deepest fears and sorrow, that we make the deepest spiritual experience— within that tension between the yin and the yang.

In the tension between contrasts we discover our true identity, but these contrasts are sometimes blurred. The truth and the fake can only be discerned by the awakened mind.

A large portion of the daily information intake is designed to appeal to the emotions of fear, greed, lust and hate. It is why education in schools on the use of social and digital media is so important.

We live in an age where we can confine ourselves to an information cocoon where we access only that information that confirms a fixed belief system, be it true or false. Doom and conspiracy prophets have always been around, feeding on basic human fears. But their outreach and capability of doing great harm is today reaching a global audience.

The awakened mind is the mind that is constantly practicing control of thoughts. Are the horses of toxic emotions running wild or do I have the ability to rein them in before they cause havoc?

Does your day control you or do you control your day? Are you setting the agenda or are external forces setting your agenda?

Alignment of body and mind is a discipline that can be practiced and will over time improve your life on multiple levels.

The Essentials:

- Elevation to higher consciousness comes when there is deep honesty and humility of heart.
- Be aware of symbols in your surroundings and your dreams.
- We cannot believe until we have experienced.
- Deepest spiritual experience comes when we transmute our deepest fear and sorrow.
- Practice control of thought.
- An awakened mind cannot be manipulated.

Chapter 29

Preparation

Preparing body and mind for a pilgrimage hike is crucial. Mental preparation starts with clarity on your sense of purpose and desire. What has inspired you to go for the walk? Are you mentally and physically in shape? Are you seeking accolades or a deeper sense of purpose?

If you are seeking spiritual meaning it is advisable to start with a regular daily meditation. Clear the mind of distracting thoughts. Focus on your breathing. Align your body with heaven and earth. As you practice your higher self will guide you and give you clarity of purpose.

Many pilgrims say the wish to do the Camino starts with a vague thought that grows into a deep desire.

You can start your research by reading one of the countless books on the Camino. The actual experience, however, will always be different. Every individual approaches the adventure from a different angle.

I did my first walk on the spur of the moment without any major preparation and would not recommend this to anyone. My boots and backpack were sub-standard. I did no prior exercising and had to experience firsthand the old Camino saying:

"Be humble or the path will humble you."

Some pilgrims have followed the ancient tradition by starting the walk from the doorstep of their home, spending months on the road.

But most who do the walk the first time or have little time start by walking the short 120-kilometer route (74 miles) from Sarria to Santiago. It will give the hiker a first inkling of the Camino.

Far more profound and life-changing is a walk lasting several weeks. It takes at least a week to wind down and to get the body adapted to a daily walk of more than 20 kilometers (12.4 miles), another week to completely immerse in the experience and another week to gradually set the thoughts on what comes when getting back home.

Joe, a hiker from California with a history of health issues, started training with baby steps, walking the five kilometers from his home to the local supermarket with his wife picking him up by car.

After some weeks of practicing Joe noticed that he was feeling healthier and fitter so that he could do the return trip of his daily walk, making it a total of ten kilometers. Then he took his backpack with him for additional training.

In keeping with his training schedule Joe after a while felt comfortable in walking the 800 kilometers (500 miles) on the Camino de Santiago. He told me he was doing fine after the first few days but then suffered bouts of severe exhaustion from walking a good 20-25 kilometers (12-15 miles) each day. Some sections demanded steep climbing up mountains and then going downhill on rock-strewn trails.

"I had to accept that I was no longer a young man and that I needed to listen carefully to my body," he said. After recuperating for a day or two he was fine again.

I have been surprised at how many pilgrims walking the Camino in

Spain each year come unprepared for the mental and physical obstacles that inevitably arise.

Even fit young hikers regularly fall prey to blisters and other physical ailments by walking too fast or too much in the first few days.

Some get horribly lost by missing a way marker or choose the wrong time of the year, underestimating the cold winds and rain in the winter months.

Authorities have closed the mountain route from St. Jean-Pied-de-Port to Roncesvalles between November 1 and March 31 after several serious accidents and loss of life in snow and fog.

In summer temperatures can soar to well over 35 degrees Celsius, especially in the Meseta after passing the city of Burgos.

Almost every year there are reports of a pilgrim dying of a heat stroke, despite the warning notifications in many of the albergues, or hostels, informing pilgrims to avoid walking in the midday heat. Most Spaniards spend the time between 1 and 5 pm taking a siesta or afternoon nap, shaking their heads in disbelief at pilgrims with heavy backpacks walking in the heat.

I would always recommend that people with a history of health issues get themselves checked by a medical doctor before they start their walk.

There are no rules telling you to walk the entire route with a heavy backpack, especially if you are in pain or cannot carry a heavy load because of a back or shoulder problem. Taxis will ferry your luggage to the next hostel or hotel destination for only a small fee.

However, every hiker should carry enough water. Drinking water from taps or streams should be avoided at all costs. Pilgrims have suffered severe diarrhea as a result, scuttling any attempt at further walking.

Testing your equipment prior to the walk is crucial. The backpack should feel comfortable, with the weight evenly distributed on the shoulders and hips. Hiking boots and socks should be of a high quality and worn-in prior to any longer walk.

Ideally you should not carry more than ten percent of your own body weight. Most people pack too much stuff on their first walk, believing still that they have reduced the weight in their backpack to the essentials. This packing list serves as a rough guideline:

Equipment:

- 40-45 liter backpack, preferably with a built-in poncho for rainy days.
- High quality hiking boots at least one size bigger than your feet.
- Trekking pants that can be zipped into short pants
- Three T-shirts, of which at least one should be long-sleeved.
- Trekking underwear that is quick-drying; one for wearing and one for washing for the next day.
- A hat for protection against the heat and sunburn.
- Two-three pairs of hiking socks.
- Rain jacket.
- Sleeping bag not weighing more than 900-1000 grams.
- Ultra-light trekking towel. Avoid at all costs cotton towels as they become very heavy when wet.
- Lightweight flipflops for the evenings after taking a shower.

Toiletry items

- Apart from basic items like toothbrush and shampoo, a tube of handwashing cream is useful to do your daily washing.
- A washing line and pegs.
- Foot care products such as an anti-blister stick and blister plasters are essentials.
- A small tube of sun cream.
- Earplugs if you are sensitive to snoring.
- Magnesium tablets, vitamin and fruit bars, aspirin or other medication you might need.

Technology

- A Spanish SIM card if your cell phone provider is from outside the European Union and doesn't make provision for roaming.
- Adapter for European electric sockets.

Documents

Documents such as ID, airline tickets and passport should be kept in a separate waterproof pouch along with your money and credit cards. Make a photocopy of your passport that you can store separately. An absolute must is health insurance for abroad that covers treatment and possible repatriation.

The Credential or pilgrim passport can mostly be obtained from the St. James Confraternities in your home country. The credential is the document that gives access to the albergues, or pilgrims' hostels, and defines your status as a pilgrim. In order to obtain the "compestela"—the document certifying your walk—you have to present the credential at the Pilgrims' Office in Santiago with all the stamps collected daily along your walk and providing a detailed record of your Camino.

I have found keeping a diary of my most valuable experiences and impressions an important tool to reflect on the Camino experience weeks or months later. The gist of conversations with fellow pilgrims have crowned my Camino experience in so many ways and inspired me to write my first Camino book: *Walking on Edge*.

Guide books are an important source of information, especially on accommodations along the route. But you should buy the latest editions and also check the Internet for updated information. I've often found an albergue recommended in a guide book to be closed or of a substandard quality. New private hostels and hotels are constantly opening along the route as the popularity of walking the Camino increases year by year.

Chapter 30

After the Journey
the Journey Begins

We are at a crucial juncture as a species. Decisions made in the next decade are likely to determine whether we will survive as a species on this planet. A key is reconnecting to the spiritual self that creates awareness and mindfulness for all living beings.

Awareness toward higher consciousness is a lifelong day-to-day challenge, while a pilgrimage to Santiago can only be one path of many.

A pilgrimage or a retreat is seldom a path toward instant enlightenment. The real journey begins after the Camino, when fundamental experience is digested.

A German pilgrim described her arrival back home:

186 | DEEP WALKING

"I was hardly back home when I broke down. Everything seemed so strange. Everyone was going about their business and I just couldn't find my place anymore. I just felt incredibly alone."

Getting back into the rhythm of a daily routine is something that many of the pilgrims find hardest after doing a Camino.

Consistency is the key. Going on a 20-kilometer (12 mile) hike each day for several weeks will have catapulted you to a fitness level and sense of well-being that you will not want to lose.

Staying consistent with good habits is all it takes. But remaining disciplined with a daily exercise routine, prayer ritual or visualization sequence is also one of the most difficult things to do.

It is the reason why highly-disciplined sports stars fall into obesity when they retire from professional play or highly successful business people lose touch with important clients and fall into a downward spiral.

Becoming a better human being is a life-long undertaking. We wouldn't be here if our soul didn't have to learn something.

Looking at the shadow and training to be compassionate, kind, humble, forgiving and grateful demands constant mindfulness.

The inability to remain consistent is one of the main reasons why most New Year's resolutions fail before the month of January has passed. Often the goals are set too high or the motivation does not come out of a deeper sense of meaning.

- Make your goal achievable so that you will have a greater motivation to start immediately rather than think about it.
- Your mindset is crucial. If you believe in yourself you can do it! If you approach it with an underlying thought of "I won't be able to do it anyway," you will fail before even having started.
- Subconsciously you might be blocked by the fear that the change in your life will be too much to handle.
- Identify the obstacles that are blocking you and find a way to get around them.

- Schedule a time slot and place in your daily routine where you consistently commit to your plan. The best time is first thing after getting up in the morning.
- Find a group, a friend, or spouse who will positively support you.

Small changes, daily positive habits, done consistently over time, in the end lead to a positive outcome.

There is the tale of an old Indian chieftain telling his grandson the story of two wolves constantly struggling in the heart of the human:

"There is the wolf of darkness, who is full of envy, desperation, fear and anger. The other is the wolf of light. It is the wolf of love, generosity, compassion, kindness and joy."

The grandson asks, "And which of the two wolves is going to win?"

Sighing, the old chieftain replies, "The wolf you choose to feed."

The Camino is a spiritual journey and it can be a homecoming to the discovery of self but complete estrangement from a life previously lived.

A gateway toward a new state of consciousness has been entered, from which there is no turning back.

The world out there and most of the time we ourselves are constantly labeling the "self" with external titles and roles: "I am a teacher, a doctor, a businesswoman, an actress, a parent."

Discovering soul identity means a radical change to the external life. Pilgrims have been known to realign their lives completely, leaving unfulfilling jobs, dysfunctional relationships or even moving to a different country.

On the Camino a label is irrelevant. You are simply a "peregrino," or pilgrim on the path, bearing your backpack and doing your daily walking like everyone else.

A label or title is mostly far removed from soul identity but we often confuse the two. When soul identity is crying out for attention it will show in fundamental restlessness born out of a feeling of inner loneliness.

Life will tug, pull and teach us lessons or gently push us forward until we hear the voice of our true soul nature. Finding our soul nature is like a homecoming.

This is when we realize that we are in complete flow with our higher purpose, our destiny, creativity and unconditional love.

We cannot, however, escape the human condition. There are circumstances that will always remain outside our control. But we have been given one great gift by the Universe that can be both a curse and a blessing. We have been given the power of choice.

A walk on the Camino starts by taking the first step and then just keeping going. At the end of the day you are amazed that you have walked more than 20 kilometers and at the end of the week more than a hundred. By the eighth week you will have walked the entire route of more than 800 kilometers

At the end of your journey you will look back at the days when you walked easily and reached the pinnacles of mountain paths with spectacular views of the mist-covered villages below. You will remember also the difficult days, the pain of blistered feet, despair, exhaustion and loss of willpower. But you raised yourself from the dust and continued.

You passed beautiful meadows with the sound of bleating sheep in your ears. You walked on hard tarmac with heavy-duty trucks thundering past only inches from your body.

You got lost and found your way again. There were beautiful mornings with rainbow colors glistening from cobwebs in the grass and there were days when your body was drenched by heavy rain and battled the midday searing heat.

It was a long road of ups and downs. You were exhilarated and you were exhausted, yet you continued, just kept walking. Was it a good journey? Was it all worth it? You bet!

You know now that there is no guide book, movie or documentary to replace the experience of doing it all by yourself. Others may walk with you but you will be walking alone for most of the time.

You bond with people who walk with you for a while and then depart. You meet new people or you may meet a person who walks with you all the way.

But you know now that giving up was never an option. You faced your fears and doubts by becoming peaceful, no matter what life throws at your feet.

You learned that on your next journey you will take less clutter. You will have a lesser load to carry and your journey will be so much easier.

You will study and plan your journey much better. You will know that you will never really be alone. You will meet new people, walk together in silence, laugh together, listen, and talk.

You trust fully in the power of the universe that you are guided and protected while walking in unknown territory.

Everything is grace when you find God's expression in your actions.

Opportunity calls with every step.

About the Author

Reino Gevers left his home country South Africa for Europe in 1981. He worked for many years as a journalist for an international news agency in Hamburg, Germany. His first book, *Wende am Kap*, published in German in 1991, deals with the author's return to his home country South Africa during the tumultuous political transition after the release of Nelson Mandela. His first fictional book, *Walking on Edge*, is based on first-hand experience during several hikes on the ancient paths of the Camino de Santiago in northwestern Spain. Reino is based on the Mediterranean island of Majorca from where he runs a health consultancy business.

CPSIA information can be obtained
at www.ICGtesting.com
Printed in the USA
JSHW011217210720
6810JS00002B/31

9 781642 798296